Adobe Edge Quickstart Guide

Quickly produce engaging motion and rich interactivity with Adobe Edge Preview 4 and above

Joseph Labrecque

BIRMINGHAM - MUMBAI

Adobe Edge Quickstart Guide

Copyright © 2012 Packt Publishing

All rights reserved. No part of this book may be reproduced, stored in a retrieval system, or transmitted in any form or by any means, without the prior written permission of the publisher, except in the case of brief quotations embedded in critical articles or reviews.

Every effort has been made in the preparation of this book to ensure the accuracy of the information presented. However, the information contained in this book is sold without warranty, either express or implied. Neither the author, nor Packt Publishing, and its dealers and distributors will be held liable for any damages caused or alleged to be caused directly or indirectly by this book.

Packt Publishing has endeavored to provide trademark information about all of the companies and products mentioned in this book by the appropriate use of capitals. However, Packt Publishing cannot guarantee the accuracy of this information.

First published: March 2012

Production Reference: 1010312

Published by Packt Publishing Ltd.
Livery Place
35 Livery Street
Birmingham B3 2PB, UK.

ISBN 978-1-84969-330-1

www.packtpub.com

Cover Image by Asher Wishkerman (a.wishkerman@mpic.de)

Credits

Author
Joseph Labrecque

Reviewer
Christer Kaitila

Acquisition Editor
Wilson D'souza

Technical Editor
Vishal D'souza

Project Coordinator
Joel Goveya

Proofreader
Martin Diver

Indexer
Rekha Nair

Production Coordinator
Alwin Roy

Cover Work
Alwin Roy

About the Author

Joseph Labrecque is primarily employed by the University of Denver as Senior Interactive Software Engineer specializing in the Adobe Flash Platform, where he produces innovative academic toolsets for both traditional desktop environments and emerging mobile spaces. Alongside this principal role, he often serves as adjunct faculty, communicating upon a variety of Flash Platform solutions and general web design and development subjects.

In addition to his accomplishments in higher education, Joseph is the Proprietor of Fractured Vision Media, LLC a digital media production company, technical consultancy, and distribution vehicle for his creative works. He is founder and sole abiding member of the dark ambient recording project "*An Early Morning Letter, Displaced*" whose releases have received international award nominations and underground acclaim.

Joseph has contributed to a number of respected community publications as an article writer and video tutorialist and is author of the *Flash Development for Android Cookbook*, Packt Publishing (2011), *What's New in Adobe AIR 3*, O'Reilly Media (2011), *What's New in Flash Player 11*, O'Reilly Media (2011), and co-author of *Mobile Development with Flash Professional CS5.5* and *Flash Builder 4.5: Learn by Video*, Adobe Press (2011).

He regularly speaks at user-group meetings and industry conferences such as Adobe MAX, FITC, D2W, 360|Flex, and a variety of other educational and technical conferences. In 2010, he received an Adobe Impact award in recognition of his outstanding contribution to the education community. He has served as an Adobe Education Leader since 2008 and is also an Adobe Community Professional.

Visit him on the web at `http://josephlabrecque.com`.

> Thanks to my family, friends, and benefactors for your continued support.

About the Reviewer

Christer Kaitila, B.Sc., is a veteran video game developer with 17 years of professional experience. A hardcore gamer, dad, dungeon master, artist, and musician, he never takes himself too seriously and loves what he does for a living: making games!

A child of the arcade scene, he programmed his first video game in the eighties, long before the Internet or hard drives existed. The first programming language he ever learned was 6809 assembly language, followed by BASIC, Turbo Pascal, VB, C++, Lingo, PHP, JavaScript, and finally ActionScript. He grew up as an elite BBS sysop in the MS-DOS era and was an active member of the demoscene in his teens. He put himself through university by providing freelance software programming services for clients. Since then, he has been an active member of the indie game development community and is known by his fellow indies as Breakdance McFunkypants.

Christer frequently joins game jams to keep his skills sharp. Over the years, he has programmed puzzle games, multiplayer RPGs, action titles, shooters, racing games, chat-rooms, persistent online worlds, browser games, and many business applications for clients ranging from 3D displays for industrial devices to simulations made for engineers.

He is the author of the book *Adobe Flash 11 Stage3D, Molehill, Game Programming Beginner's Guide*, and is about to publish *Game Jam Survival Guide*.

He runs a popular news website called www.videogamecoder.com, which boasts over 30,000 articles and zero ads. He is one of the Administrators of Ludum Dare. His client work portfolio is available at www.orangeview.net and his personal game development blog is www.mcfunkypants.com, where you can read more about the indie game community and his recent projects.

He lives in Victoria, Canada with his beloved wife and the cutest baby son you've ever seen.

www.PacktPub.com

Support files, eBooks, discount offers and more

You might want to visit www.PacktPub.com for support files and downloads related to your book.

Did you know that Packt offers eBook versions of every book published, with PDF and ePub files available? You can upgrade to the eBook version at www.PacktPub.com and as a print book customer, you are entitled to a discount on the eBook copy. Get in touch with us at service@packtpub.com for more details.

At www.PacktPub.com, you can also read a collection of free technical articles, sign up for a range of free newsletters and receive exclusive discounts and offers on Packt books and eBooks.

http://PacktLib.PacktPub.com

Do you need instant solutions to your IT questions? PacktLib is Packt's online digital book library. Here, you can access, read, and search across Packt's entire library of books.

Why Subscribe?

- Fully searchable across every book published by Packt
- Copy and paste, print, and bookmark content
- On demand and accessible via web browser

Free Access for Packt account holders

If you have an account with Packt at www.PacktPub.com, you can use this to access PacktLib today and view nine entirely free books. Simply use your login credentials for immediate access.

Table of Contents

Preface	**1**
Chapter 1: Introduction to Adobe Edge	**5**
Why we need Adobe Edge	**5**
Flash Player restrictions	5
The relationship between Adobe Edge and Adobe Flash Professional	7
Comparisons with Adobe Flash Professional	7
Stage	7
Timeline	8
Keyframes	8
Symbols	8
Library	9
Actions	9
HTML technology maturity	10
Mobile deployment	10
What Adobe Edge can be used for	**11**
Web animation	12
Interactive content	12
The history of Adobe Edge	**12**
The inner workings of Edge	**13**
HTML, CSS, and JavaScript	14
HTML	14
CSS	14
JavaScript	14
How jQuery is used in Edge	15
JSON	15
The Adobe Edge Runtime	16
Getting started	**16**
Installing Adobe Edge	16
The Adobe Edge welcome screen	18
Creating a new Edge Project	19

Save	20
Save As...	21
Edge project file structure	21
Summary	**23**
Chapter 2: The Edge Application Interface	**25**
Application interface overview	**25**
The application window	26
Customizing the Edge panel layout	26
Managing workspaces	27
The Edge menu system	**29**
File	30
Edit	31
View	32
Modify	32
Timeline	33
Window	35
Help	36
The Edge Toolbar	**36**
Selection tool	37
Transform tool	38
Rectangle tool	39
Rounded Rectangle tool	40
Text tool	41
Background Color and Border Color	42
The Stage	**42**
The Edge Timeline	**44**
Panels in Edge	**44**
Elements panel	45
Library panel	46
Properties panel	47
Actions panel	48
Summary	**49**
Chapter 3: Working with Edge Tools and Managing Assets	**51**
Using the drawing tools	**51**
The Rectangle tool	52
Using the Rectangle tool	52
The Rounded Rectangle tool	53
Using the Rounded Rectangle tool	54
The Text tool	56
Using the Text tool	57
Using web fonts	60

The Selection and Transform tools	62
Using the Selection tool	63
Color tools	69
Importing external assets	**69**
What is SVG?	69
Importing SVG images	71
What is a bitmap?	72
Importing bitmap Images	73
Working with imported assets	75
Converting assets into symbols	**75**
Create a Symbol	76
Summary	**77**
Chapter 4: Creating Motion with Edge	**79**
Animation within Edge	**79**
The Edge Timeline	**80**
Playback controls	80
Time	80
Search	81
Timeline options	81
Timeline controls	81
The Playhead	82
The Mark	82
Zoom controls	83
Keyframes	83
Creating motion	**84**
Animating with the Playhead	84
Animating with the Mark	86
Editing Transition	88
Duration	89
Delay	89
End	89
Easing	89
Example: Animating a website header	90
Project setup, asset import, and general layout	90
Animating elements	92
Summary	**94**
Chapter 5: Adding Interactivity to an Edge Composition	**95**
Working with Actions	**95**
The Timeline Actions layer	96
Working with Triggers	96
Working with Labels	97
Applying Actions to the Stage	98
Applying Actions to individual elements	99

Overview: The Adobe Edge Runtime APIs	**100**
Document Object Model events	101
Mouse events	101
Touch events	102
Virtual mouse events	102
Timeline events	103
Example: Adding interactivity to a website header	**104**
Creating the Text element	104
Adding interactivity to the Title	106
Adding interactivity to the album art	106
Completing the final website header composition	108
Summary	**109**
Chapter 6: Additional Resources	**111**
Using an Edge composition within an existing website	111
Online resources	112
About the forthcoming book: Learning Adobe Edge	114
Learning Adobe Edge	115
Robust motion and interactivity through web standards	115
Index	**117**

Preface

Edge is an all-new tool from Adobe (currently in pre-release) that seeks to enable the authoring of motion and interactive experiences through HTML, CSS, and JavaScript in a manner consistent with other Creative Suite applications. The Edge application shares many features with other Adobe products, particularly Flash Professional, After Effects, and InDesign. This book will detail how to use this professional authoring software to create highly engaging content that targets Web standards. Content created in Adobe Edge does not rely on a plugin, so it can be run within any standard browser, even on mobile devices. The goal of this quickstart guide is to provide a direct overview of what it takes to create engaging content for the Web and provide a level of familiarity with Edge in order to actually get it done!

What this book covers

Chapter 1, Introduction to Adobe Edge, provides a look at the shifting Web landscape and how changes within devices and browser capabilities have made it possible for Adobe Edge to come about as a useful tool in the field of web design and development.

Chapter 2, The Edge Application Interface, provides a comprehensive overview of the entire Edge application interface. This overview includes a look at the panels, tools, menus, and other application elements that we will need to familiarize ourselves with when using Edge.

Chapter 3, Working with Edge Tools and Managing Assets, delves into many of the tools contained within the Edge application to allow the creation of rectangular elements, text, and assorted other objects.

Chapter 4, Creating Motion with Edge, demonstrates how simple it is to build a composition that involves a number of animated elements and presents a unique toolset for dealing with motion on the Web.

Preface

Chapter 5, Adding Interactivity to an Edge Composition, will expand upon the motion-based topics of *Chapter 4* through the addition of interactive elements within an Edge project.

Chapter 6, Additional Resources, provides additional resources, which are available over the Internet and also seeks to add a few tips and tricks not covered in the preceding chapters. We close out with a preview of the forthcoming comprehensive book *Learning Adobe Edge, Packt Publishing*.

What you need for this book

To use this book effectively, the reader will need to download the Adobe Edge Preview from Adobe Labs. This is a free download and Adobe is releasing regular updates to the preview along the way to the release version of the application.

Adobe Edge Preview can be acquired from: `http://labs.adobe.com/technologies/edge/`

Who this book is for

This book is for anyone who wants to get started using Adobe Edge to create engaging and interactive content for the Web. It isn't necessary for the reader to have any prior knowledge of website or motion design.

Conventions

In this book, you will find a number of styles of text that distinguish between different kinds of information. Here are some examples of these styles, and an explanation of their meaning.

Code words in text are shown as follows: "These elements will default to a `<div>` HTML element, but can be changed to employ the following HTML elements instead."

A block of code is set as follows:

```
(function(symbolName) {
Symbol.bindElementAction(compId, symbolName, "${_fvm001}",
"mouseover", function(sym, e) {
// Change an Element's contents.
//   (sym.$("name") resolves an Edge element name to a DOM
//   element that can be used with jQuery)
sym.$("Info").html("August (2000)");
});
```

When we wish to draw your attention to a particular part of a code block, the relevant lines or items are set in bold:

```
Symbol.bindElementAction(compId, symbolName, "${_Rectangle}",
"vmousedown", function(sym, e) {
sym.playReverse();
// insert code for vmousedown here
});
//Edge binding end
```

New terms and **important words** are shown in bold. Words that you see on the screen, in menus or dialog boxes for example, appear in the text like this: "Now we will perform the preceding exercise, but this time will employ the **Mark** to demonstrate an alternate way of creating motion in Edge".

> Warnings or important notes appear in a box like this.

> Tips and tricks appear like this.

Reader feedback

Feedback from our readers is always welcome. Let us know what you think about this book—what you liked or may have disliked. Reader feedback is important for us to develop titles that you really get the most out of.

To send us general feedback, simply send an e-mail to feedback@packtpub.com, and mention the book title through the subject of your message.

If there is a topic that you have expertise in and you are interested in either writing or contributing to a book, see our author guide on www.packtpub.com/authors.

Customer support

Now that you are the proud owner of a Packt book, we have a number of things to help you to get the most from your purchase.

Downloading the example code

You can download the example code files for all Packt books you have purchased from your account at http://www.packtpub.com. If you purchased this book elsewhere, you can visit http://www.packtpub.com/support and register to have the files e-mailed directly to you.

Errata

Although we have taken every care to ensure the accuracy of our content, mistakes do happen. If you find a mistake in one of our books—maybe a mistake in the text or the code—we would be grateful if you would report this to us. By doing so, you can save other readers from frustration and help us improve subsequent versions of this book. If you find any errata, please report them by visiting http://www.packtpub.com/support, selecting your book, clicking on the **errata submission form** link, and entering the details of your errata. Once your errata are verified, your submission will be accepted and the errata will be uploaded to our website, or added to any list of existing errata, under the Errata section of that title.

Piracy

Piracy of copyright material on the Internet is an ongoing problem across all media. At Packt, we take the protection of our copyright and licenses very seriously. If you come across any illegal copies of our works, in any form, on the Internet, please provide us with the location address or website name immediately so that we can pursue a remedy.

Please contact us at copyright@packtpub.com with a link to the suspected pirated material.

We appreciate your help in protecting our authors, and our ability to bring you valuable content.

Questions

You can contact us at questions@packtpub.com if you are having a problem with any aspect of the book, and we will do our best to address it.

1
Introduction to Adobe Edge

Edge is an all-new tool from Adobe (currently in pre-release) which seeks to enable the authoring of motion and interactive experiences through HTML, CSS, and JavaScript in a manner consistent with other Creative Suite applications. Edge has the ability to create such experiences, due to advancements in browser technology and the need for a consistent, cross-platform solution across desktop and mobile operating systems. Over the course of this book, we will explore the basics of motion and interactivity in this new tool.

This chapter will delve into Adobe Edge itself, concentrating on the history of the Edge project, looking at the technologies behind Edge, comparing Edge with Flash Professional (as the two applications share many similarities), and finally having a brief look at the Edge welcome screen and how to create a new project.

Why we need Adobe Edge

Some may ask for an explanation as to why we need Edge when we have tools such as Flash Professional, which also creates animation and interactive contents for the web. There are a number of reasons for this, which we will now illustrate.

Flash Player restrictions

Traditionally, those of us designing animated or highly interactive content for the web have been able to rely on Flash Player to display this content without issue across Windows, Mac, and Linux. In fact, Adobe still reports that Flash Player is installed on 99% of desktop machines. There are problems though, now that we must account for mobile operating systems, which place restrictions upon, or even outright ban the Flash Player entirely. The most problematic of these platforms is Apple iOS. As Flash content is restricted from running within the iOS browser, designers have been searching for alternative ways of delivering experiences to these devices.

Introduction to Adobe Edge

 It is worth noting that the Google Android and Blackberry QNX mobile operating systems both have robust Flash Player 11 support. However, Adobe has halted any further development for the mobile Flash Player after version 11.1. Others do have the option of licensing Flash Player and integrating it into their systems, as RIM continues to do for their QNX-based systems such as Blackberry 10 smartphones and PlayBook tablets.

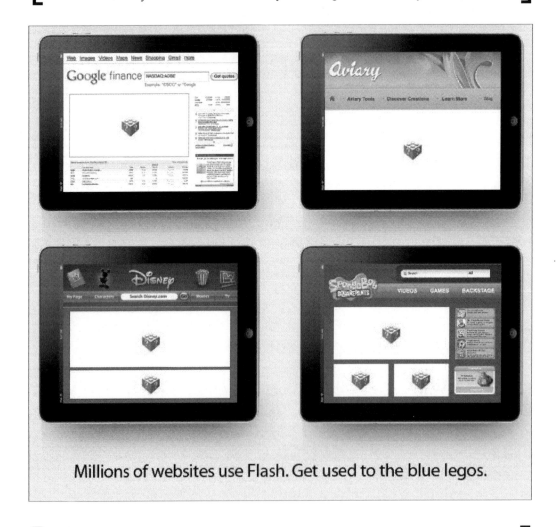

Millions of websites use Flash. Get used to the blue legos.

 Though Apple iOS has banned Flash Player in the browser, Flash content can be distributed through the Apple App Store in the form of compiled applications, which target this platform. Similarly, other mobile operating systems such as Google Android and RIM Blackberry QNX also include full support for Flash-based projects through Adobe AIR.

The relationship between Adobe Edge and Adobe Flash Professional

Depending on the type of project we are working with, Edge might be considered as a competing product to Flash Professional. If we are looking to create a website landing page, rich menu system, or advertisement—then yes, Edge is definitely a competitor to Flash Professional. However, it is important to recall that Adobe produces many different tools, which produce similar output; just look at Photoshop and Fireworks for an obvious example of this.

When evaluating Edge in comparison to Flash Professional, we must take into account how new Edge and the concepts around it actually are. Flash Professional has over 15 years of history behind it. It is unrestrained by standards bodies and has a track record of rapid innovation when pushing web-based content beyond what HTML is traditionally capable of. Flash also benefits from compiling to a self-contained binary (.swf) and the powerful ActionScript 3 programming language.

While Flash Professional and Edge can do some things in a similar way, and can produce similar output in terms of motion and basic interactivity, for anything that goes beyond what HTML can handle on its own, Flash-based content is still a powerful extension for console-quality games, advanced video solutions, and other specific use cases.

Comparisons with Adobe Flash Professional

With the expectation that many designers approaching Edge will be coming to it with experience in Flash Professional, much of the tooling in Edge shares both functional and naming conventions used in that application.

Stage

The Stage can be thought of as the canvas upon which we are able to paint our scenes, or the frame within which all our action takes place. The Stage in Edge differs from the one in Flash in the way that its dimensions are controlled and the background color is applied. In Edge, the Stage is just another symbol.

Timeline

Flash Professional and Edge do share the concept of a Timeline; that is where the similarities end. The Flash timeline is frame-based while Edge includes a time-based timeline, similar to what is found in Adobe After Effects. In the end, these are just two ways of working with motion across time—in essence, this is what we are dealing with in either case.

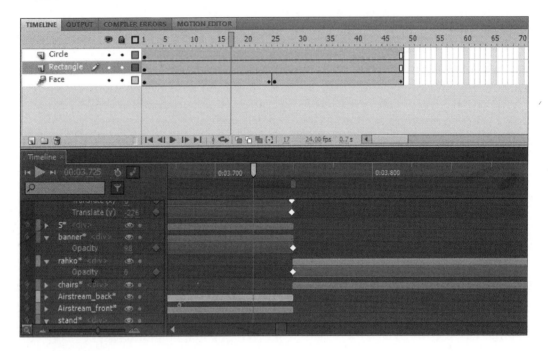

Keyframes

Both Flash Professional and Edge give the user the ability to define keyframes across the project Timeline. Keyframes are points of distinction that define or modify various properties of an element across time. This is the most basic way in which motion is achieved in either program. Keyframes in Edge behave to a great degree such as those from Adobe After Effects.

Symbols

Symbols are reusable assets, whose instances can be used across a project. In Flash Professional, these may be movieclip, button, or graphics symbols. In Edge, there is no such distinction; though Edge symbols are most similar to Flash movieclip symbols in execution.

Chapter 1

Library

Flash Professional organizes Symbols, Fonts, and Assets within a project Library. The Library panel is an organizational approach that provides easy access to the symbols. With Edge, we have a similar concept that also stores any symbols created for a project within that project's Library, exposed through the Library panel.

Actions

Actions in Edge can be compared with those in Flash Professional (*Macromedia Flash 4*). Each program has an Actions panel, which can be opened and closed as needed to access simple program instructions. In Edge, we can apply Actions to elements on the stage, and to the Timeline through Triggers.

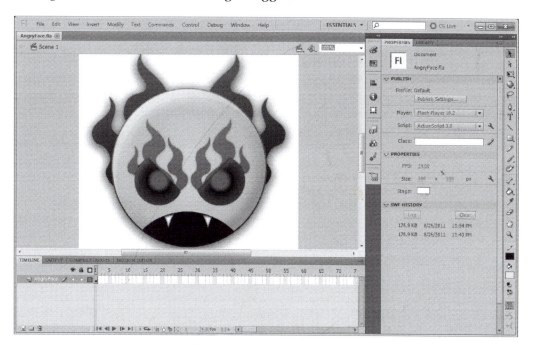

As we can see from the previous screenshot, many of the panels present in Edge are derived from those which exist in Flash Professional. This makes the transition much simpler for Flash designers than it would otherwise be.

HTML technology maturity

For much of its history, HTML has provided a way for web designers to creatively markup content for rendering within a browser. With the draft HTML5 specification currently under development, this role has been expanded in some ways, which attempt to move beyond simple textual markup and into the rich-media space.

Three tags often cited as examples of this are:
`<video>` - for simple video playback in HTML
`<audio>` - for simple audio playback in HTML
`<canvas>` - for programmatically rendering bitmap visuals in HTML through JavaScript APIs

Along with the core HTML specification, in development are a variety of additional specifications such as CSS3 that are intended to extend the core technologies of the web. We have also seen a great increase in the speed of JavaScript engines over the past couple of years, enabling greater use of the basic scripting language for the web. Add a number of frameworks (such as the popular jQuery [http://jquery.com/] framework) to this environment and we have quite a revolution in core web technologies.

Mobile deployment

Perhaps the single largest driving factor in the rapid evolution of core web technologies over the past two years has been the prevalence of advanced browsers on mobile devices. Due to the fact that mobile computing is still so new, users are not coming into this environment with old technology. This enables browser makers and device manufacturers to bundle web browsers with these systems that takes full advantage of HTML5, CSS3, and advanced JavaScript rendering engines.

Most mobile browsers are based upon the open source WebKit [http://www.webkit.org/] rendering engine. Couple this with the fact that prominent desktop browsers such as Google Chrome and Apple Safari also use WebKit for their rendering engines, and we have a widely adopted baseline to lean upon when developing experiences using newer technologies.

What Adobe Edge can be used for

Generally, Edge can be used to create many of the same types of animations and interactions that we would have expected Flash Player to handle on the web in the mid to late 1990s. This includes the movement of visual objects across the stage and basic mouse interactions.

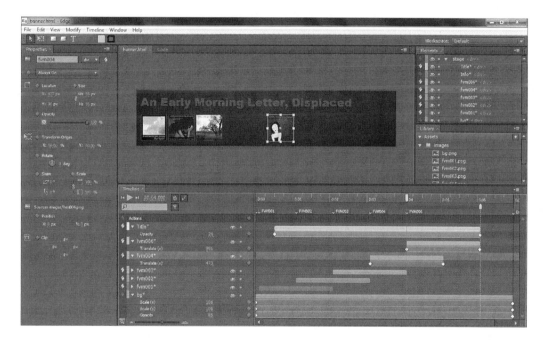

 Although it is now possible to create website intros, rich ads, and other motion content using a tool such as Edge, designers should be careful not to replicate the nuisances of the past. The web doesn't need more "Skip Intro" landing pages.

Web animation

Edge uses an all-new timeline for producing motion which borrows a lot from other applications such as Adobe After Effects. Through the use of keyframes along the Timeline, designers have very fine-grained control over many object properties and can easily enable easing algorithms, which provide an additional flair to animated content. In many ways, the Edge Timeline is superior to that found in other animation programs due to the level of control a designer is provided, and how richly control over these properties is enabled through the tools.

Interactive content

Edge is not just about making things move. The Edge Runtime also includes a robust API to enable interactivity through mouse, touch, and time-based Actions. These interactive commands can be applied to individual visible objects upon the stage, or used along the Timeline in the form of Triggers. Interactivity can modify aspects of the stage Timeline, modify the properties of other objects within an Edge project, or even invoke calls to content outside of the project.

The history of Adobe Edge

During the 2010 Adobe MAX conference in Los Angeles, California, Adobe engineers got on stage in front of over 5,000 attendees to present a software prototype built in Adobe AIR. This software allowed a user to adjust the properties of imported assets in a way very similar to the workflow of Flash Professional, but instead of outputting to SWF to target the Flash Player, the "Adobe Edge Prototype" actually output content to HTML, CSS, and JavaScript for playback in a web browser without the need for any additional plug-ins.

Adobe AIR is a solution for creating desktop and mobile applications built on Flash Platform technology. Many Adobe products are built using AIR, including the new touch applications for use on Android tablets.
http://www.adobe.com/products/air.html

Chapter 1

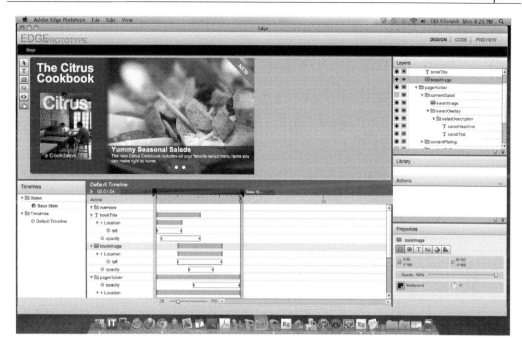

This was the first glimpse of what would eventually become the product we know today as Adobe Edge. Since that time, Adobe has released periodic updates to the "Adobe Edge Preview" releases on Adobe Labs with the intention of gathering user feedback early and often in order to make the product conform to user expectations and become a useful addition to the Creative Suite.

With Adobe's long history of motion and interactivity in products such as Director, After Effects, and Flash Professional, Edge has an excellent lineage behind it; and while creating such content which targets HTML is quite new, the tools and techniques for authoring this material comes to us along a well-trodden and mature path.

The inner workings of Edge

Adobe Edge relies heavily on three related technologies: HTML, CSS, and JavaScript. There are also specific JavaScript libraries that play an essential role in making all of this work together. These include **jQuery** and the **Adobe Edge Runtime**. In order for Edge content to work successfully, all of these components must be in their correct place, and there are certain files which should not be edited once generated by the application. The Edge application itself also requires an .edge file type to be present in order to author and edit a project.

Note that any `.html` file can also be opened up within Edge and be worked upon. An `.edge` file and associated imports will be created upon saving and publication.

HTML, CSS, and JavaScript

Edge primarily targets HTML for display, supported by both CSS and JavaScript. Why? Well, the fact is that these technologies have finally become capable of handling rich motion and interactive content and as they are the core technologies of the web, it really only makes sense to use them whenever we can.

Let's have a quick look at these three specifications in light of their primary function on the web and relation to one another.

HTML

Hyper Text Markup Language is the core of the web. With the HTML5 specification (still in draft), we not only have an organic evolution of the language through additional semantic tags, but also a new set of APIs, which can allow elements within the documents to be greatly influenced through JavaScript.

CSS

Cascading Style Sheets determine to a great extent how a website is visually structured and designed. With the CSS3 specification (still in draft), designers can also be used to influence the way certain elements behave.

JavaScript

The JavaScript language is a superset of ECMAScript (ECMA-262) Edition 3, formalized by ECMA International, a worldwide standards body. The latest version of the language is JavaScript 1.8.5 but the real improvements in recent years have come from the browser manufacturers themselves, as they seek to improve JavaScript execution through the development of faster JavaScript engines.

When we look into an HTML document produced by Edge, we see the following:

```
<div id="stage" class="EDGE-937066003">
</div>
```

This is the Stage Symbol element within which all other elements are injected upon runtime, through the use of JavaScript libraries.

> Note that this is the only HTML element you will ever see produced by Edge. Everything else is handled via JavaScript Object Notation (JSON) objects and specialized JavaScript includes.

How jQuery is used in Edge

It is no exaggeration to state that jQuery is the most popular JavaScript framework in use today. Many similar JavaScript frameworks arose in 2007 with the emergence of AJAX (Asynchronous JavaScript and XML) and more dynamic HTML data transfer methods. At one point, there existed over 250 of these frameworks, but with the passing of time, only a handful remains in active development.

As stated on the project website, jQuery is a fast and concise JavaScript Library that simplifies HTML document traversing, event handling, animating, and AJAX interactions for rapid web development. In a nutshell, jQuery aims to make JavaScript more tolerable, more consistent across browsers, and more powerful in its simplicity. Documentation for jQuery can be found online at http://docs.jquery.com/.

Adobe Edge leverages jQuery and builds upon it within the "Adobe Edge Runtime" and also makes use of the jQuery library when dealing with motion. When opening any HTML generated by Edge, we can see these includes in the head of our published document.

> Note that other Adobe products, such as Adobe Dreamweaver, also make heavy use of jQuery. In fact, Adobe actively contributes back to the jQuery and jQuery Mobile libraries.

JSON

JavaScript Object Notation is a data-interchange format used to exchange data from one system to another. Over the past few years, it has been adopted by a variety of languages and systems for both data transmission and storage. In some ways, it is very similar to XML. Unlike XML, JSON is not a markup language but rather stores data in objects and structures represented in name/value pairs.

Edge uses JSON to store element definitions and attributes with a project. For example, the following JSON fragment represents a red rectangle on the stage:

```
content: {
  dom: [
  {
    id:'Rectangle',
```

```
        type:'rect',
        tag:'div',
        rect:[117,56,185,185],
        fill:['rgba(192,192,192,1)'],
        stroke:[0,"rgba(0,0,0,1)","none"]
        }],
    symbolInstances: [
    ]
 },
```

To learn more about JSON visit http://www.json.org/.

The Adobe Edge Runtime

The set of JavaScript libraries used in an Edge project is collectively referred to as the "Adobe Edge Runtime". Normally, when we think of a runtime, we are talking about a piece of software such as Flash Player, the Adobe Integrated Runtime (AIR), or the Java Runtime Environment. These are all self-contained pieces of software that enable the playback of applications and other content, which targets these specific runtimes. The Adobe Edge Runtime is very different in that it is a set of files that supports the content defined through the Adobe Edge application, but even these libraries rely upon another piece of software for them to run properly: the web browser.

If you look within an HTML file produced by Edge, you will see a JavaScript include, which handles the runtime libraries included within the head of that document.

```
<!--Adobe Edge Runtime-->
<script type="text/javascript" charset="utf-8" src="BasicEdgeProject_
edgePreload.js"></script>
<!--Adobe Edge Runtime End-->
```

Getting started

Before moving on, we'll want to be sure that Adobe Edge is installed and running properly on our system. We'll also have a brief look at the Edge interface and see how to create a new project.

Installing Adobe Edge

To complete the demonstrations and examples included in this book, you'll need to acquire a copy of Adobe Edge itself. Edge can be installed as a trial from Adobe Labs. To download a trial version of Edge, you may use the following URL: http://labs.adobe.com/technologies/edge/

Adobe Edge can be installed on the following systems:

- Microsoft Windows 7
- Apple Mac OS X [10.6]

> Note that installing Edge on Microsoft Windows XP or Apple Mac OS X [10.5] are not supported in any way.

Once the Edge installer has been downloaded to your local machine, locate the installer and execute it using the usual method for your specific operating system.

The installer will initialize, during which we must **ACCEPT** the software license agreement.

We are then able to install a trial version. As this is a pre-release product, we cannot input a valid serial number.

The final screen will allow us to make some choices about where exactly the installer will install Edge on our local machine, and the language that will be installed. We are also presented with an indication of how much space Edge will occupy once it has been installed upon a particular machine.

Clicking **FINISH** will complete the installation process using the choices we have made. It may take a few minutes for the installation to complete, depending upon your individual hardware setup.

We are now ready to begin using Adobe Edge. Locate the start up icon on your machine to run the application.

Introduction to Adobe Edge

The Adobe Edge welcome screen

When starting the Adobe Edge application, we'll be presented with a welcome screen. This is very similar to the welcome screens available in other Adobe applications, as it presents a number of options for us to get started using the product.

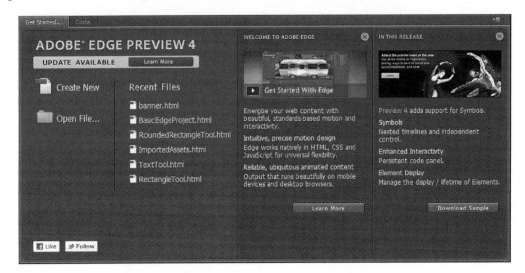

These options include the following:

- **Create New**: This option will enable us to create a brand new Edge project. We will detail the specifics of this in the next topic.
- **Open File...**: When we choose this option, a local filesystem browse dialog will open for us. This allows us to browse the filesystem to locate Edge projects that are already under construction. Edge documents have the file extension .edge.
- **Recent Files**: Any Edge projects that were previously opened within the application will be listed under this option. Opening these projects is as simple as clicking upon the project name.

- **Other options**: The welcome screen also includes some social-media buttons that allow users to connect with the Edge team on Facebook and Twitter. There are also resources listed for learning how to get started using Edge for those who are new to the application, and sample projects, which we can download.

Creating a new Edge Project

There are two ways in which we can create a new Edge project. The first option is to simply click **Create New** on the welcome screen. This will immediately create a new Edge project with a blank stage. The second method of creating a new Edge project is through the **File** menu. Simply clicking on **File** and then **New** will have the exact same effect.

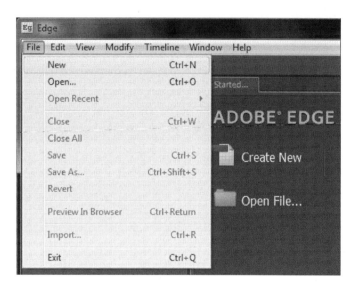

Introduction to Adobe Edge

Whichever method you choose, you will now have a new project opened within Edge. This project will look quite scarce to begin with, as it basically consists of a single, blank stage symbol. This stage is representative of the single `<div>` that we can locate within the HTML file, which Edge produces upon saving.

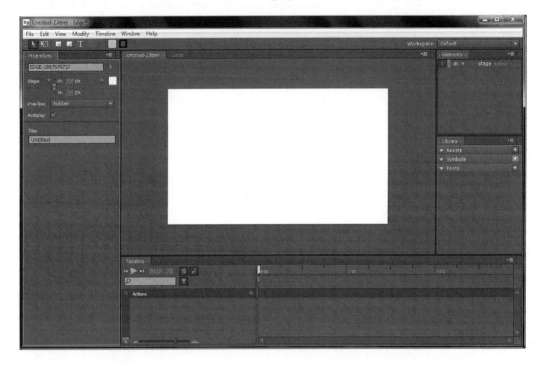

After our project has been created, the first item of business is to actually save the document.

To save a document in Adobe Edge, we can go to the **File** menu and choose either the **Save** or **Save As...** options.

Save

This option will either save the current document, if it has been previously saved to the filesystem, or it will prompt the user to provide a filename and location to save the document if this happens to be a new project.

The keyboard shortcut for this option is *Ctrl+S* (Windows) or *Command+S* (Mac).

Save As...

Similar to the **Save** option, this provides the same functionality but will always prompt the user for a filename and location through a system dialog. This is useful when saving separate versions of the same project, or when you simply want to save the project to a new location.

The keyboard shortcut for this option is *Ctrl+Shift+S* (Windows) or *Command+Shift+S* (Mac).

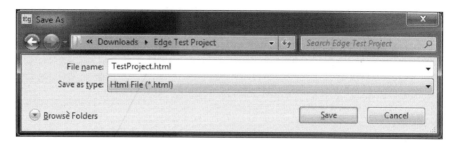

In the case of a new project, either option will provide us with a filesystem dialog. We see from the previous screenshot that what we are actually saving is an `.html` file. This is an important thing to remember about Edge projects: when we are working in the Edge authoring environment, we are really working in real time with the content that is being produced.

Edge project file structure

As we save our Edge project, a number of files are produced and included in the location we specified when naming the initial `.html` file. We'll have a look at each of these files, and what their specific purpose is within our project.

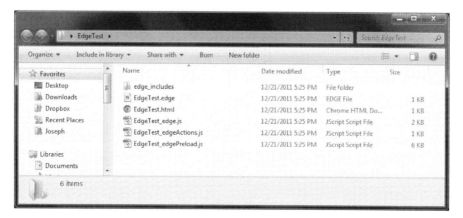

- `{project_name}.edge`: The `.edge` file produced along with the project simply preserves properties within the authoring environment. Examples of these properties include whether certain elements are twirled down through the Elements panel, specific colors, and fonts used in the project. This file allows environment settings to be preserved across sessions.
- `{project_name}.html`: The `.html` file serves many purposes. It is the file used within an Edge project that serves to bind all of the Edge Runtime and project-specific files together. This is also the file that is effectively opened within the authoring environment. Finally, running this file in a browser allows us to preview our full project.
- `{project_name}_edge.js`: This is actually a file containing all of the JSON structures associated with an Edge project, along with some code that binds the Edge stage to a specified HTML element and initializes the runtime.
- `{project_name}_edgeActions.js`: This JavaScript file contains all of the Actions defined within the Edge application.
- `{project_name}_edgePreload.js`: This JavaScript file serves to load in all of the other files and bind them to the project upon runtime. There is also the groundwork in Adobe Edge Preview 4 for composition preloaders, but this is not yet complete.
- `edge_includes`: This directory contains the jQuery and Adobe Edge Runtime files necessary for the proper working of the project. None of the files within this directory should ever be modified manually.
    - `jquery-{version}.min.js`: This is the minimized jQuery library packaged along with the Edge Runtime.
    - `jquery.easing.{version}.js`: This is the minimized jQuery easing library packaged along with the Edge Runtime.
    - `edge.{version}.min.js`: This is the minimized Adobe Edge Runtime library.
    - `yepnope.js`: This is asynchronous conditional resource loader to manage the assets that need to be loaded based upon the client environment. Read more about it at: `http://yepnopejs.com/`

Summary

In this chapter, we had a look at some ways in which the web landscape is changing, specifically when talking about the roles of the primary technologies used to create motion and interactive design in the browser. The content produced by Edge would only have been possible using Flash Player in years past. HTML, CSS, and JavaScript have advanced to the point where this sort of content can now be produced using core web technologies. At the same time, Adobe Flash Player and the wider Flash Platform have expanded beyond these roles.

We have also taken a look at the history behind the Adobe Edge application from its beginnings as a basic prototype and have looked into a number of the standard web technologies used by Edge projects. We also discussed Edge in relation to Adobe Flash Professional and many of the similarities between the two programs. If you are used to Flash Professional, picking up Edge is relatively simple!

Finally, we had a brief look at Edge itself, including how to install the program, the options available to us using the Edge welcome screen, and how to quickly create a new Edge project.

2
The Edge Application Interface

Adobe Edge boasts a modern, designer-friendly user interface that should be somewhat familiar to longtime users of the Adobe Creative Suite applications. This chapter will run through each aspect of the interface, including:

- Interface features
- Application menus
- The Toolbar
- The Stage
- The Timeline
- Edge panels

After processing the information presented, we should have a clear understanding of the interface as a whole and also the usefulness of individual aspects.

Application interface overview

Being primarily focused on motion and interactivity, the Edge interface places a great emphasis upon modifying element properties over time. We will discover that Edge places many useful sections of the interface such as the **Stage**, **Timeline**, and **Properties** panels in plain view in order to make these tools readily available in our work.

The application window

Whether running Edge on Windows or OS X, the application window will appear very similar across platforms. In many of Adobe's creative products, the windowing on OS X is very different than it is on Windows. With Edge, the operating mode is the same across platforms; so while the reader will notice most of the screenshots in this book featuring from the Windows version of Edge, there should be very little difference when running the application on OS X.

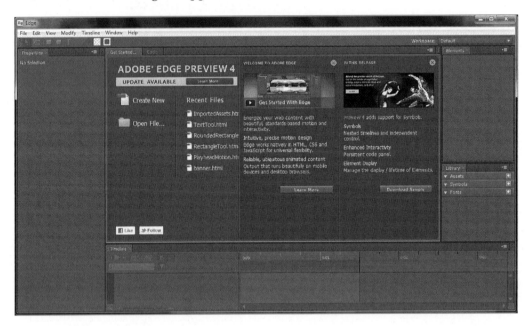

The application window itself is broken into a variety of separate modules. Most of these modules fall under the category of "panels" and can be toggled on and off, collapsed, combined with other panels, or anchored to different areas of the application window. Most of these actions are done through mouse actions and dragging.

Customizing the Edge panel layout

Any panel in Edge can be anchored to the application window or can be made to float within a small utility window. Floating panels are useful if placing them across different monitors on a full workstation, whereas docking these panels can preserve space on a smaller laptop display.

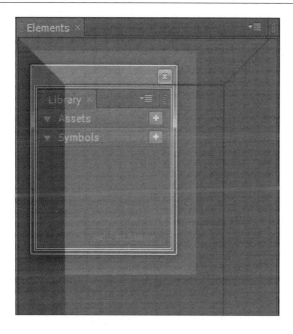

To tear a panel out of the main application window and create a floating panel, simply click upon the grippies (the textured area of the panel tab) next to an anchored panel's name. While the mouse button remains pressed, pull the panel from its present location. We will see the panel has now changed state.

At this point, as we move our cursor among other interface elements, we will see a grid appear from time to time with portions of the grid highlighted in a violet color. This color indicates that the panel may be dropped in this location to be anchored in that particular position. Release the mouse button to dock the panel, or release it when there is no highlighted portion of the grid to allow the panel to remain in a floating state.

 Dragging a panel totally off of the application window and releasing it will ensure that we create a floating panel.

Managing workspaces

In a similar fashion to other Creative Suite applications, Edge provides the ability to customize the workspace and preserve a variety of these customizations through the concept of application workspaces.

The Edge Application Interface

The ability to easily switch between different workspaces is useful when moving between the layout, animation, and interactivity portions of a project, as the relevant panels and other interface structures can be given more prominence, and those which are not needed for certain tasks can be either dismissed or placed in a smaller role.

To create a new workspace, we will perform the following actions:

1. First, locate the **Workspace** drop-down in the upper-right portion of the Edge application window. Click on it to reveal the drop-down choices.

2. Select **New Workspace** and provide a Name for your custom workspace. Select **OK** once you are finished.

3. To verify that your workspace has been saved, return to the **Workspace** drop-down and click on it once again. Your new workspace will appear in the list of choices. Switching between workspaces is now as simple as performing a quick selection using this drop-down control.

Chapter 2

We have a few other options for managing our workspaces apart from **New Workspace**. We also have **Delete Workspace**, which deletes the currently selected workspace from memory. Also useful is the ability to reset a workspace that has been modified by choosing the **Reset "{workspace}"...** option. In case, while working, we have modified our workspace to assist with a particular task the reset option allows us to quickly revert to our saved workspace instead of manually moving things back to how they were.

The Edge menu system

Most computer programs have a standard menu system that includes choices such as **File**, **Edit**, and **View**, along with a variety of application-specific choices. Edge is no different in this regard.

We will have a look at the options available to us from the Edge application menu and provide a brief overview of the function of each option.

File

The **File** menu option provides a number of options for working with Edge files themselves.

- **New**: Creates a new, blank Edge project.
- **Open**: Opens a previously saved Edge project.
- **Open Recent**: Provides a list of recently opened Edge projects that a user can select from. Selecting one of these projects will load it into Edge, similar to the **Open** command.
- **Close**: This command will close the current Edge project, prompting the user to save the document first, through an application alert window.
- **Close All**: Closes all Edge projects that are currently open. Similar to the **Close** command, a dialog box requesting the user to save each project will appear in a sequence.
- **Save**: Saves the current Edge project. Only valid for previously saved projects.
- **Save As...**: Opens a browse dialog prompting the user to provide a project file name and location to save the Edge project. Previously unsaved projects are required to use this command.
- **Revert**: Reverts an opened and modified Edge project to its last saved state.
- **Preview In Browser**: While it is possible to preview certain things within the Edge application itself, as projects become more complex, we will want to be sure and run them within a true browser environment. This command will launch a browser and load in the current Edge project automatically.
- **Import...**: Allows the import of .png, .gif, .jpg, and .svg files into an Edge project. These imported files will appear in the project **Library** and upon the stage.
- **Exit**: Closes the entire application. If there are unsaved projects open, Edge will prompt the user to save the document first, through an application alert window.

Edit

The **Edit** menu allows for direct object manipulation through cut, copy, and paste commands, along with selection options, and access to an undo/redo history.

- **Undo**: Reverts the previous action. This command will change based upon context, letting the user know precisely which action will be affected.
- **Redo**: Reverts the previous **Undo** command. This command will change based upon context, letting the user know precisely which action will be affected.
- **Cut**: Removes the selected element. The user may decide to **Paste** this element elsewhere.
- **Copy**: Copies the selected element. The user may decide to **Paste** this element elsewhere.
- **Paste**: Pastes the previously cut or copied element onto the stage while preserving element properties such as position, opacity, rotation, and so forth.
- **Paste Special**: This is actually a series of commands which allows the pasting of specific attributes. Similar to any **Paste** command, these attributes or an accompanying element must have been cut or copied previous to this.
    - **Paste Transitions To Location**: Will replicate the exact motion from the copied element upon the selected element. The Transition will terminate upon the elements present position.
    - **Paste Transitions From Location**: Will replicate the exact motion from the copied element upon the selected element. The Transition will begin at the elements present position.
    - **Paste Inverted**: Will paste an inverted (or reverse) sequence of what has been copied or cut into the Timeline.
    - **Paste Actions**: Will paste only the Actions defined on the element that has been copied or cut to a new element.
    - **Paste All**: Will paste the element which has been copied or cut as a new element along with all properties, Actions, and Transitions into the Timeline.
- **Duplicate**: Makes a perfect copy of the selected element. All properties and attributes are preserved and the original object is left intact.
- **Select All**: Selects everything on the stage.
- **Delete**: Removes the selected element from the stage without preserving the object for a **Paste** command in the future.

View

Commands from the **View** menu determine how the stage appears within the application window.

- **Zoom In**: Zooms in the entire stage for fine adjustments when placing objects or modifying their properties. If the stage appears larger than its panel, scrollbars will be present.
- **Zoom Out**: Zooms the stage out further. Useful if working on smaller, cramped screens.
- **Actual Size**: Resets the stage to its actual size as given in the Properties panel.

Modify

The **Modify** menu includes commands that pertain to elements on the stage and how the stage interacts with these elements. Most of these commands pertain to layout and distribution options, but also particular commands, which deal with the management of Symbols.

- **Arrange**: The arrangement commands modify the z-index of visual elements on the stage.
    - **Bring to Front**: Switches the selected element z-index position to the very top of the viewing stack.
    - **Bring Forward**: Switches the selected element z-index position to the spot above its current position within the viewing stack.
    - **Send Backward**: Switches the selected element z-index position to the spot below its current position within the viewing stack.
    - **Send to Back**: Switches the selected element z-index position to the very bottom of the viewing stack.
- **Align**: This set of commands adjusts the x or y positions of selected elements with one another.
    - **Left**: Aligns selected elements to the left-most element.
    - **Horizontal Center**: Aligns selected elements to their horizontal center.
    - **Right**: Aligns selected elements to the right-most element.
    - **Top**: Aligns selected elements to the top-most element.
    - **Vertical Center**: Aligns selected elements to their vertical center.
    - **Bottom**: Aligns selected elements to the bottom-most element.

- **Distribute**: These commands adjust the x or y positions of selected elements to one another.
    - **Left**: Distributes selected items along the left edge.
    - **Horizontal Center**: Distributes selected items along the horizontal center.
    - **Right**: Distributes selected items along the right edge.
    - **Top**: Distributes selected items along top edge.
    - **Vertical Center**: Distributes selected items along vertical center.
    - **Bottom**: Distributes selected items along the bottom edge.
- **Enable Smart Guides**: Enables smart guides to appear when dragging elements around the stage. Smart guides assist in the alignment of items in relation to one another.
- **Convert to Symbol...**: Converts the selected elements on the stage into a new symbol, allowing us also to provide the symbol with a name through a simple dialog.
- **Edit Symbol**: If a symbol has been selected, Edge switches the view to an isolation mode within that symbol in order to edit its contents.

Timeline

As Edge is a motion- and animation-focused tool, the following **Timeline** commands listed are core to achieving the most we can through the application interface.

- **Play/Pause**: Toggles playback of the timeline.
- **Move Playhead to Start**: Sends the timeline playhead to 0 milliseconds.
- **Move Playhead to End**: Sends the timeline playhead to the very end of the established timeline.
- **Auto-Keyframe Properties**: Setting this will enable Edge to generate keyframes for various properties automatically as they are adjusted along the timeline.
- **Generate Smooth Transitions**: Informs Edge to use smooth transitions between element property adjustments.
- **Insert Label**: Adds a label marker at the current playhead position. The label name can be edited.
- **Insert Trigger**: Adds a new trigger to the Actions layer along the timeline at the current playhead position.

- **Insert Time**: Invokes a dialog that allows the insertion of time extending from the current playhead position along the timeline. This will extend the overall timeline length as well.
- **Toggle Mark**: Toggles the mark on and off, depending upon particular preferences when animating elements.
- **Snapping**: Toggles snapping on and off.
- **Snap To**: Specifies the snapping settings when snapping has been toggled on.
    - **Quarter Seconds**: Snap to quarter seconds along the timeline
    - **Playhead**: Snap to the playhead position
    - **Transition Edges**: Snap to transition edges
- **Zoom In**: Scales the stage in from its current scale.
- **Zoom Out**: Scales the stage out from its current scale.
- **Zoom to Fit**: Scales the stage to fit within constraints imposed by the size of the application window.
- **Expand/Collapse Selected**: Expands selected elements within the timeline to expose their individual keyframes.
- **Expand/Collapse All**: Expands all elements within the timeline to expose their individual keyframes.

The following screenshot is an example of a Timeline menu:

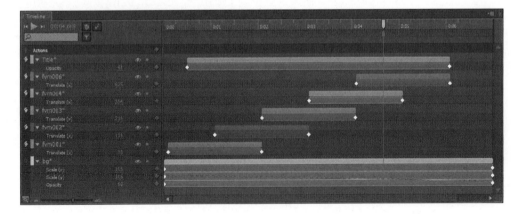

Window

The **Window** menu provides the ability for an Edge user to toggle various application panels on and off. The following screenshot is of a Window menu:

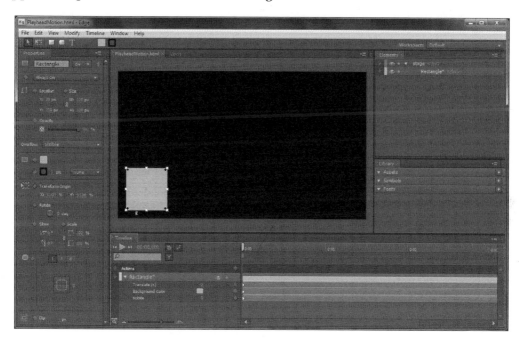

Certain panels are off by default; turning them on will allow us to anchor them to the application window, or otherwise position them as floating panels. In this menu, we are also given access to workspace management commands.

- **Workspace**: Provides a number of commands for managing Edge workspaces.
    - **Default** (also listed are any defined workspaces): These are simply quick access commands to switch between defined workspaces.
    - **New Workspace**: This command will save the current application window configuration as a named workspace for later recall.
    - **Delete Workspace**: Deletes the currently selected workspace from application memory.
    - **Reset "{workspace}"...**: This command allows us to quickly revert to our saved workspace to its saved state.
- **Timeline**: Toggles the Timeline within the Edge application window.
- **Elements**: Toggles the Elements panel within the Edge application window.

The Edge Application Interface

- **Editor**: Currently disabled in Edge Preview Release 4.
- **Library**: Toggles the Library panel within the Edge application window.
- **Tools**: Toggles the Tools panel within the Edge application window.
- **Properties**: Toggles the Properties panel within the Edge application window.
- **Code**: Currently disabled in Edge Preview Release 4.

Help

This menu item contains information about Edge as a product, and links to information about the APIs which exist when interacting with the runtime through JavaScript.

- **About Product Improvement Program...**: An opt-in to allow the user to participate in improving the product through the collection of anonymous usage statistics.
- **About Adobe Edge...**: Selecting this will bring up information about Edge, including specific version information.
- **About JavaScript API...**: Provides an overview of the Adobe Edge Runtime API (requires an Internet connection).

The Edge Toolbar

The Edge **Toolbar**, by default, is located along the top left of the application window and contains an assortment of tools used when interacting with the stage. In this toolbar, we will discover a selection tool, vector element creation tools, and a text tool for working within the Edge Stage.

 Each Adobe Edge Preview has added a significant amount of new features to the application. We can expect that the **Toolbar** may also continue to improve with time.

Selection tool

The **Selection** tool appears as a little cursor arrow and is used to make selections upon the project stage. Any elements added to the stage can be selected using this tool and holding down the *Shift* key, a user can toggle the selection of multiple elements at once.

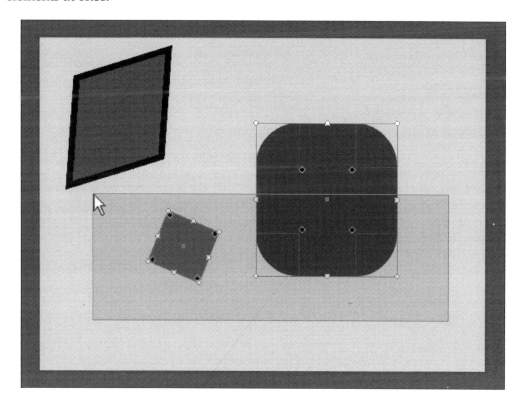

A user is also able to draw a selection box across elements by clicking upon an area of the stage that includes no other elements and dragging across multiple elements before releasing the mouse. This will draw a selection rectangle during the selection process, which will go away once a selection has been completed.

 Once objects are selected, they can be modified in many different ways through the use of panels and menu systems within the Edge application window.

Transform tool

The **Transform** tool allows us to modify certain transform properties through direct manipulation of the object on the stage. There is a subtle difference, between the **Transform** and **Selection** tools, but it is a very important one. When using the **Transform** tool to modify an element, we are modifying transform properties in relation to the **Transform Point**, while the **Selection** tool can modify only properties such as width and height. The following is a screenshot of the Transform tool:

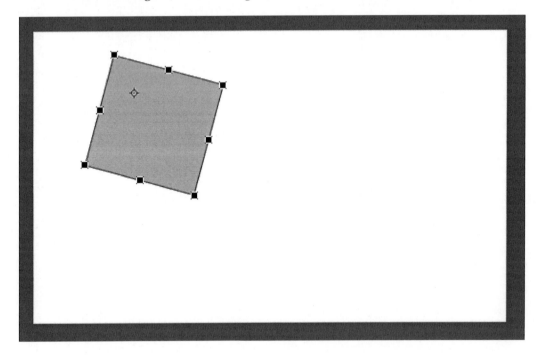

 The **Transform Point** can be moved anywhere within the element or even outside of the element to create a number of interesting motion effects.

Rectangle tool

The **Rectangle** tool looks similar to a small rectangle in the **Toolbar**. Selecting this tool allows us to create rectangular elements directly upon the stage. To create a new rectangle using this tool, we click upon the stage and drag the mouse across the area we wish the rectangle to appear over, finally releasing the mouse once we are finished. Holding the *Shift* key down while dragging out our rectangle will allow us to create a perfect square.

[After a rectangle has been created, we can manipulate the small black diamonds at each corner to form a rounded rectangle.]

Rounded Rectangle tool

The **Rounded Rectangle** tool is almost identical to the **Rectangle** tool, except for the fact that it will retain the border radii settings from one instance to another as new rounded rectangles are created.

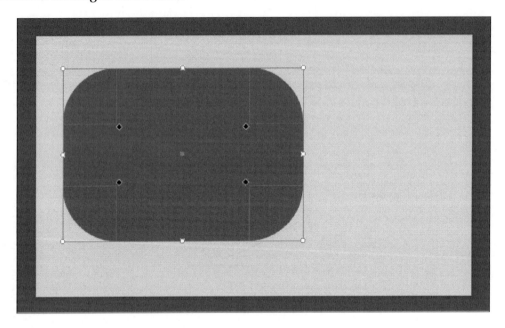

 As is the case with the **Rectangle** tool, after a rounded rectangle has been created, we can further manipulate the small black diamonds at each corner to adjust the border radii.

Text tool

Using the **Text** tool, we are able to define text elements within an Edge project and modify certain visual properties of that element. We can choose to either click upon a location on the stage and begin typing or click and drag a textbox to whatever size is needed.

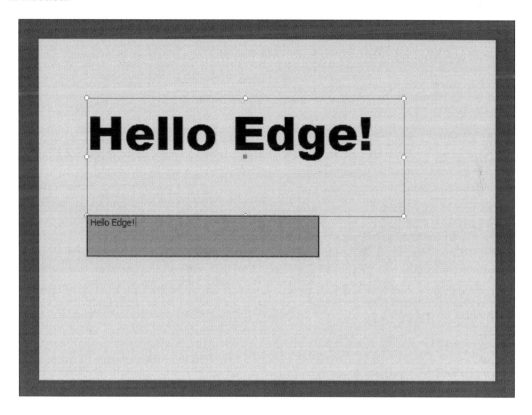

 As well as by using these tools, any of the specific element properties can also be adjusted and changed through the **Properties** panel.

Background Color and Border Color

This simply provides quick access to both element background and border color selectors from the Edge application **Toolbar**.

Normally, this can also be modified through the **Properties** panel when an element has been selected.

The Stage

The **Stage** in an Edge project is the fundamental starting point of our element structure. Any additional elements created or imported will reside within and be animated upon this stage.

The stage itself is actually just another Symbol within Edge. The element which represents the Stage is the only HTML element, which can be seen when viewing the source code of the .html file produced by Edge.

```
<!DOCTYPE html>
<html>
<head>
<title>Untitled</title>
<!--Adobe Edge Runtime-->
<script type="text/javascript" charset="utf-8"
  src="BasicEdgeProject_edgePreload.js"></script>
<!--Adobe Edge Runtime End-->
</head>
<body style="margin:0;padding:0;">
<div id="stage" class=" EDGE-3551296988">
  </div>
</body>
</html>
```

Downloading the example code

You can download the example code files for all Packt books you have purchased from your account at http://www.packtpub.com. If you purchased this book elsewhere, you can visit http://www.packtpub.com/support and register to have the files e-mailed directly to you.

The stage element for any particular Edge project will always have a unique class attribute, which is bound to jQuery functionality contained within the project's main JavaScript file. In the case of the previous code, the class value is EDGE-3551296988 and the JavaScript file in question is BasicEdgeProject_edge.js.

Have a look at the files within the sample BasicEdgeProject for the full project source.

Users coming to Edge from Flash Professional will undoubtedly notice some similarities, as Flash Professional also has the concept of a Stage. Though there are many differences between the two types, as in Edge, the stage is much more easily controlled through the motion engine, allowing us to resize or change the background color at will. In Flash Professional, the Stage is much more static; for instance, the background color cannot be animated in any such way as in Edge.

The Edge Application Interface

The Edge Timeline

The **Timeline** in Edge defines the various elements that are at play over time and exposes changes related to these elements in a visual way. The Edge **Timeline** is robust, yet simple to use. It inherits many of its attributes and behaviors from other applications such as After Effects and Flash Professional, yet it makes a good attempt to refine these concepts as well. The following is a screenshot of Edge **Timeline**:

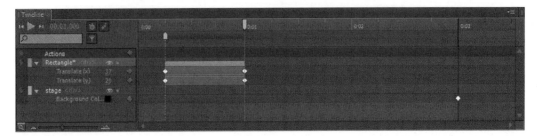

Panels in Edge

For those familiar with other applications in the Adobe Creative Suite, the concept of panels will be quite familiar. As an example, in the following screenshot, we see panels as implemented in what is perhaps one of the most popular applications in the Creative Suite: Photoshop.

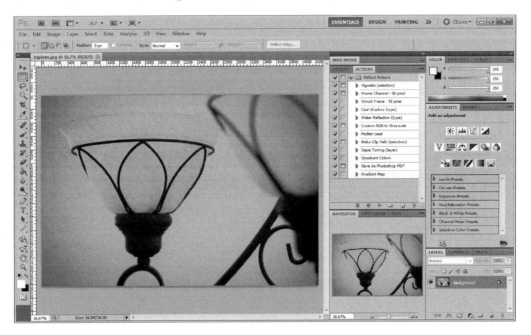

Panels are defined sets of functionality exposed through the application graphical user interface (GUI). Generally, the panels in Adobe Edge can be closed, combined, moved, resized, and collapsed as needed. Any panels that are not present in a particular workspace configuration can be opened through the **Window** menu commands.

Elements panel

The **Elements** panel is a representation of all the HTML elements included as part of our Edge project. Every element is always nested within the stage and elements, which contain sub-elements, can be twirled down to expose those elements. We may also toggle visibility of particular elements by toggling the eye icon on and off, as well as the lock icon. When an element is locked, Edge will prevent us from modifying the properties of that particular element.

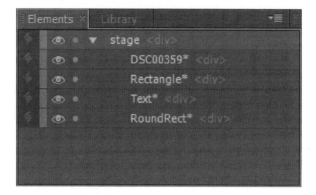

To reorder elements, we can drag-and-drop individual elements within the **Elements** panel. This will effectively modify each element's z-index accordingly.

We can also toggle the visibility of any element by clicking the eye icon to the left of the element name. Clicking the small dot next to the eye will lock a particular element, disabling editing.

Library panel

The **Library** panel includes a listing of imported **Assets** such as bitmap and SVG images, a list of **Symbols** that have been created within Edge, and **Font** definitions, which can be used through text elements. The first two of these elements are added to the **Library** panel once they are included within an Edge project and can be added to the stage from this panel. The **Font** definitions are added through this interface and then referenced through text elements within the **Properties** panel.

By clicking upon the plus button attributed to either category, we can either add a new **Asset** through a file browse dialog or create a new **Symbol** from selected elements. Web **Fonts** can also be defined through the **Library** panel in this manner.

Properties panel

The **Properties** panel is one of the most important panels within Edge, as this is where all of the properties of an element can be modified. The properties available to us will depend upon the element that has been selected. For instance, the Stage will have very few properties in comparison to a rectangle or text element. Following is the screenshot of the **Properties** panel:

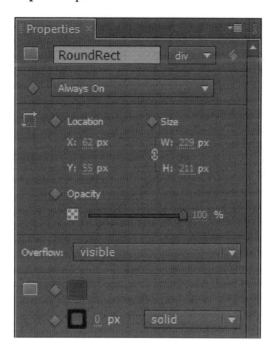

 Many of the Adobe Creative Suite applications include the concept of a properties panel. Applications such as Flash Professional, which have been inherited from Macromedia, normally feature this panel quite prominently among the various application panels.

Actions panel

The **Actions** panel in Edge allows us to insert small bits of JavaScript code into our compositions. This code comes in the form of **Triggers, Events,** and **Actions**. The basic idea is that we are either able to write JavaScript in this panel, which conforms to the Edge Runtime API, or we can alternatively employ the buttons along the left side of the panel to insert preconfigured bits of code onto an element.

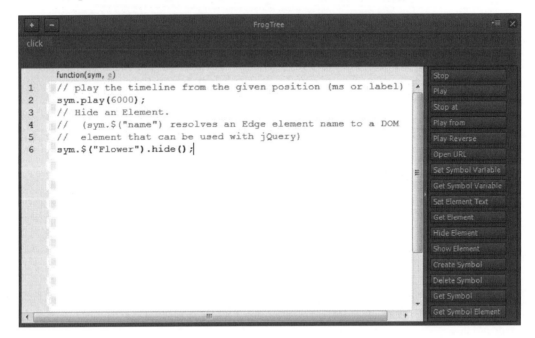

 Depending upon whether we are inserting code along the **Timeline** as a **Trigger** or upon an element or **Symbol** as an **Event** determines the options available for us in the options stack.

Summary

We should now be familiar with all of the menus, panels, and other interface elements available to us in within the Adobe Edge application window. While we have touched upon some basic functionality in this chapter, the following chapters will demonstrate a number of ways in which we can use Edge to create a variety of standards-based projects that leverage motion and interactivity to produce rich, engaging content for the web.

Next, we'll look specifically at the various tools available to us in Edge and how to import assets from other programs for use in our compositions.

3
Working with Edge Tools and Managing Assets

In order to perform any sort of animation or interactivity in an Edge composition, we'll need to either create or import the elements necessary for a particular project. In this chapter, we'll have a look at the drawing tools available to us in Edge, including:

- The Rectangle tool
- The Rounded Rectangle tool
- The Text tool
- The Selection tool
- The Transform tool
- Color tools

We'll also go through some basic examples of using these tools, and demonstrate how to import external assets into a composition. Finally, we'll see how to create **Symbols** in Edge, and define custom **Font** definitions in the **Library**.

Using the drawing tools

Edge includes a limited number of drawing tools, which can be used to create elements within our composition. These elements can eventually be made to move around, allow user interaction, or even be made into Edge **Symbols**.

The drawing tools can be accessed through a series of icons within the Edge **Toolbar**. By default, the **Toolbar** is positioned at the very top of the application window, below the application menu.

> It is possible to move the **Toolbar** around, as it is a panel and therefore shares all of the options and attributes of any panel within the Edge application interface. For more information on this, have a look at the previous chapter.

The Rectangle tool

The Edge **Rectangle** tool allows us to create rectangular elements upon the **Stage** which can be animated through the **Timeline** or have interactivity applied to them through the **Actions** panel. These elements will default to a `<div>` HTML element.

Using the Rectangle tool

To create a new element using the **Rectangle** tool:

1. Create a new Edge project and name it `RectangleTool.html`.
2. Select the **Rectangle** tool from the Edge **Toolbar**.
3. Hover over the **Stage**. Notice that the cursor now appears as a crosshair.
4. Click anywhere on the **Stage** and drag. Notice as you do, the rectangle will grow or shrink, depending upon how far you drag from your original point. When you are happy with the size of your rectangle element, release the mouse button to complete this task.

> Holding *Shift* while dragging out a new rectangle element will create a perfect square instead of a rectangle.

5. The **Selection** tool will automatically be activated for us and the rectangle element just created will be in a selected state. We can now modify the element that was just created through the **Properties** panel as shown in the following screenshot:

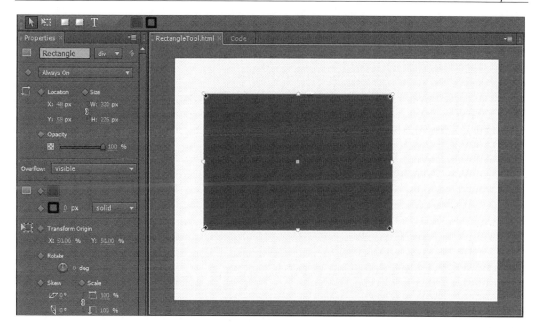

 Moving the **Transform Origin** point by clicking upon it and dragging it to a new location with the mouse will allow the rectangle element to be transformed as though pinned to this point instead of the element center.

 Files for this project are located in the RectangleTool directory.

The Rounded Rectangle tool

The Edge **Rounded Rectangle** tool allows us to create rectangular elements with rounded corners upon the **Stage**, which can be animated through the **Timeline** or have interactivity applied to them through the **Actions** panel. These elements will default to a `<div>` HTML element.

The **Rounded Rectangle** tool behaves almost exactly like the **Rectangle** tool and elements produced with either tool function identically.

Using the Rounded Rectangle tool

To create a new element using the **Rounded Rectangle** tool:

1. Create a new Edge project and name it `RoundedRectangleTool.html`.
2. Select the **Rounded Rectangle** tool from the Edge **Toolbar**.
3. Hover over the **Stage** and you will notice that the cursor now appears as a crosshair.
4. Click anywhere on the **Stage** and drag; notice as you do, the rounded rectangle will grow or shrink, depending upon how far you drag from your original point. When you are happy with the size of your rounded rectangle element, release the mouse button to complete this task.

> Just as the case with the **Rectangle** tool, holding *shift* while dragging out a new rounded rectangle element will create a square instead of a rectangle.

5. The **Selection** tool will automatically be activated for us and the rectangle element just created will be in a selected state. We can now modify the element that was just created through the **Properties** panel.

> Holding the *Ctrl* key and dragging any of the radius modifier diamonds will allow us to modify only the selected corner in isolation from the rest.

Notice that the element created with the **Rounded Rectangle** tool looks a bit different from the previous rectangle element that was created with the **Rectangle** tool. This is because the **Rounded Rectangle** tool will create, by default, a rounded rectangle element whose border radius is 10 pixels at each corner. One other attribute unique to this tool is that it will remember the previous radii settings upon subsequent use. Let's modify the settings of the element we've just created in order to demonstrate this concept.

1. With the rounded rectangle element we just created, look over at the **Properties** panel.
2. Modify the **Border Radius** to be something other than the default 10 pixels.
3. Now select the **Rounded Rectangle** tool from the Edge **Toolbar**.
4. Draw out another rounded rectangle element upon the **Stage**.

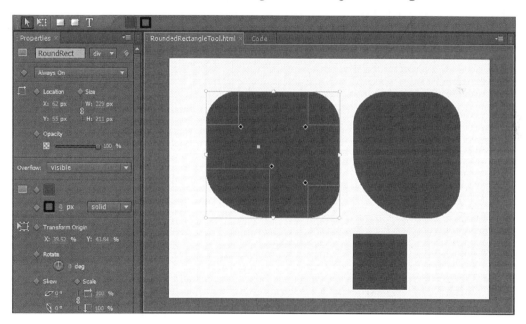

Notice that this new element retains all of the properties that were adjusted in the previous rounded rectangle element. Even if we now select the **Rectangle** tool and create some elements with that, the **Rounded Rectangle** tool will still remember the previous settings used with that tool.

Holding *Shift* and dragging any of the radius modifier diamonds will allow us to align all corner radii together while snapping to a 90-degree angle.

Files for this project are located in the `RoundedRectangleTool` directory.

The Text tool

The Edge **Text** tool allows us to create text elements upon the **Stage**, which can be animated through the **Timeline** or have interactivity applied to them through the **Actions** panel. We can also perform advanced functions such as modifying the textual contents through the application of various actions, which we will see later on in this book.

These elements will default to a `<div>` HTML element, but can be changed to employ the following HTML elements instead.

Possible text element types:

- `<div>`: Defines a division element within an HTML document and is often used for generic block-level elements.
- `<address>`: Normally added to the header or footer of an HTML document; this tag defines contact information for the document owner.
- `<article>`: Defines a block of self-contained content. Commonly used for an article or blog post.
- `<blockquote>`: An element, which defines a section of text that has been taken from a source other than the current document.
- `<p>`: Denotes a block element, which signifies a paragraph of text.
- `<h1 - h6>`: H1 – H6 are basic HTML heading tags. They can be used to denote a hierarchical set of headings within a parent element.
- `<pre>`: Denotes preformatted text. Normally, this tag will preserve whitespace and line breaks.
- `<code>`: Ideal for displaying blocks of code within HTML.

As we can see — through these element definitions — most of the differences are simply *semantic*, although semantic meaning is a core consideration when dealing with HTML-based content.

Advanced text treatments or bizarre fonts can also be rendered from an image-editing program as SVG or bitmap images and included within an Edge composition in that way.

Using the Text tool

To create a new text element using the **Text** tool:

1. Create a new Edge project and name it `TextTool.html`.
2. Select the **Text** tool from the Edge **Toolbar**.
3. Hover over the **Stage**, and notice that the cursor now appears as a crosshair.
4. Click anywhere on the **Stage** and drag. Notice that as you do so, the text element outline will grow or shrink, depending upon how far you drag from your original point. When you are happy with the size of your text element, release the mouse button to complete this task.

 Alternatively, we can simply click upon the **Stage** and begin typing using the Text tool. The text element will expand to accommodate the characters that are input.

5. The **Selection** tool will automatically be activated for us and the text element just created will be in a selected state. A small input box will appear beneath the newly formed text element, allowing us to type the text we want to be displayed.
6. Once we have finished typing our text, we can hit the *Enter* key or click off of the text element to finish. We will now be able to modify that element through the **Properties** panel.

We now have a complete text element on the **Stage** as shown in the following screenshot, which reads out the text that was entered upon its creation.

 Double-clicking upon any text element will allow us to edit the text that is displayed within that element.

Similar to the behavior of the **Rounded Rectangle** tool, the **Text** tool will retain any of the properties from its previous use. To see this behavior in action, perform the following steps.

1. Select the text element just created and look over at the **Properties** panel.
2. Modify the **Font Size** and **Text Color** to be something other than the default.
3. Now select the **Text** tool from the Edge **Toolbar**.
4. Draw out another text element upon the **Stage** using whichever method suitable to you.

Chapter 3

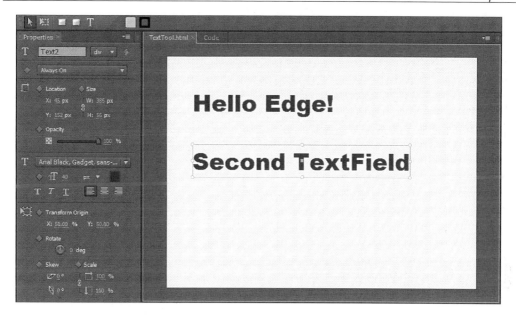

Notice that this new element retains all of the properties that were adjusted in the previous text element.

 Files for this project are located in the TextTool directory.

Using web fonts

Web fonts are externally hosted font definitions that can be defined and stored within the Library panel for use upon text elements. For this example, we will be using Google Web Fonts [http://www.google.com/webfonts], but a service such as TypeKit [http://typekit.com/] can also be employed.

To define a Font asset within the Library:

1. Go to Google Web Fonts and choose a font to use within an Edge composition.
2. Grab the linkage tag. It will look something similar to the following:
   ```
   <link href='http://fonts.googleapis.com/css?family=Flavors'
     rel='stylesheet' type='text/css'>
   ```
3. Also note the given name of the font. In this case, it is "Flavors".
4. Within Edge, go to the **Library** panel and click the **+** icon next to **Fonts**.
5. In the **Add Web Font** dialog that appears, paste in the full linkage tag copied from the font service into the **Embed Code** field.
6. Within the **Font Fallback List** input, paste the name of the font being included. We can also provide a comma-separated list of additional fonts in case there is a problem.

7. When finished, click **Add Font** to close the dialog. This font will now appear within the **Library** panel and become accessible from the internal font list when dealing with text elements.

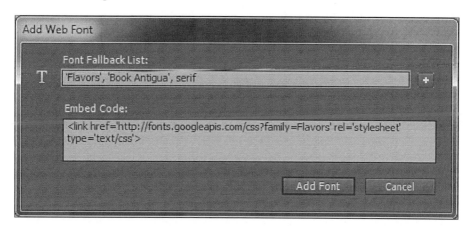

To test our new font in an Edge composition:

1. With the **Text** tool selected, click upon the **Stage**.
2. Type the following: `Custom Web Fonts ROCK!` and hit the *Enter* key.
3. In the **Properties** panel, use the Font Name drop-down to select the web font we created earlier.
4. We can now adjust additional element properties until we are happy with the outcome.

Now we have a custom web font that can be used within this project. At this time, custom font definitions cannot be shared across multiple Edge projects. They must be defined for each and every project.

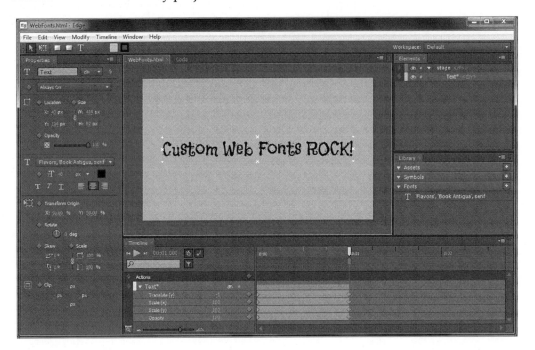

 Of course, text elements using web fonts can also be animated just like any other text element!

 Files for this project are located in the WebFonts directory.

The Selection and Transform tools

Now that we've created a number of elements on the **Stage** using these internal tools, we can have a look at the **Selection** tool and explore its usage. The **Selection** tool is used (as its name suggests) to select one or more elements on the **Stage** and modify their properties through the mouse, menu commands, keyboard commands, or the **Properties** panel. The **Transform** tool is similar to this, though when employed, will only adjust transform properties such as **Scale** and not **Size**, as is done through the **Selection** tool.

Using the Selection tool

To select an element on the **Stage** using the **Selection** tool, all we need to do is choose the **Selection** tool from the **Toolbar** and then use it to click upon the element we wish to select. This will allow us to modify the properties of this element through either movements with the mouse, through keyboard shortcuts, or most extensively, by using the **Properties** panel.

To select many elements upon the **Stage** at once, we can click-and-drag across all of the elements we wish to select. When multiple elements have been selected in this manner, the **Properties** panel will display only those properties that are shared between object types. For example, if we were to select both a rectangle and text element at once, we would be able to modify the **Location** and **Size** of both objects at once, but could not edit the **Font Size** or **Border Radius**, as these properties are specific to each object type.

We may also click upon multiple elements while holding the *Shift* key in order to select/deselect multiple objects on the **Stage**.

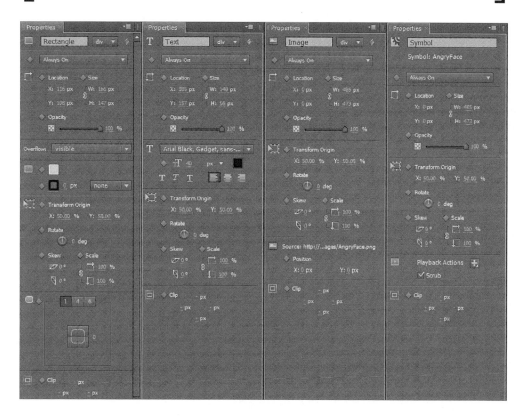

The previous screenshot illustrates the different properties available to us through the various element types available to us in Edge. Notice how many properties are shared.

Properties shared by all element types

Following are the list of properties, which can be shared by all elements:

ID

The **ID** is used throughout Edge to identify a particular element in the **Elements** panel, the **Timeline**, and also via various actions through the use of JavaScript code.

Tag

This property specifies the HTML tag to be used to define a particular element. These choices will change depending upon the element type.

Element Display

There are three choices here: **Always On**, **On**, or **Off**. If setting to **On** or **Off**, the display of the element must be managed along the **Timeline**.

Location

The **x** and **y** coordinates that an element will be positioned at on the **Stage**, in pixels.

 Unlike Flash, Edge is not capable of sub-pixel rendering.

Size

Determines the width and height of an element in pixels.

Opacity

Determines the degree of transparency exhibited by a particular element. This can range from 0 percent to 100 percent, with 100 percent being fully opaque.

Transform Origin

This is the point that any transformations such as rotation or scale will be applied from. Determined by **x** and **y** percentage values.

Rotate

Degrees of rotation of the specified element, with 0 being original rotation.

Skew

The skew of an element can be performed along either the **x** or **y** axis.

Scale

Based on percentage, both **x** and **y** scale can be linked or changed independently.

Clip

Clipping an element from the **top, bottom, left,** or **right** will render a portion of the selected element invisible from the specified side based upon the specified pixels.

Properties unique to rectangle elements

The following properties are unique to rectangle elements:

Overflow

This property determines how the rectangle element behaves when nested elements extend past its borders. There are four choices:

- **visible**: Elements that extend past the rectangle borders will remain visible
- **hidden**: Elements that extend past the rectangle borders will be rendered invisible
- **scroll**: The rectangle element will present scrollbars to the user, even if not necessarily needed
- **auto**: Elements that extend past the rectangle borders will cause scrollbars to appear automatically, as needed

Background Color

The color to apply to our rectangle background in RGBA format: Red, Green, Blue, Alpha.

Border Color

The color to apply to our rectangle border, if it exists, in RGBA format: Red, Green, Blue, Alpha.

Border Thickness

Specifies the thickness of the border, if it exists, in pixels.

Border Style

Specifies the style of border around the rectangle element. Can be set to **none**, **solid**, or **dashed**.

Border Radius

Specifies the roundness of the border radius. This property can be set to apply to all corners, individual corners, or even specific x and y properties of individual corners. It is very flexible!

Properties unique to text elements

The following are a list of properties unique to text elements:

Font Name

These are core fonts that almost every computer is expected to be able to display. They are arranged here in groups, to allow for fallback in case the primary font is not available on a user's system.

Font Size

A numeric size attributed to the chosen font. This setting functions along with **Font Size Units**.

Font Size Units

The unit of measurement of attribute to a chosen **Font Size**. Choices include **px** or **em**.

Text Color

The color to apply to our text in RGBA format: Red, Green, Blue, and Alpha.

Bold

A toggle for the chosen font's bold property. Emboldens the text.

Italic

A toggle for the chosen font's italic property. Italicizes the text.

Underline

A toggle for the chosen font's underline property. Applies a visual line beneath the text.

Align Left

Only usable in text-field elements that are given a certain width which is greater than the space occupied by the provided text. Aligns given text to the left.

Align Center

Only usable in text-field elements that are given a certain width which is greater than the space occupied by the provided text. Aligns given text to the center.

Align Right

Only usable in text-field elements that are given a certain width which is greater than the space occupied by the provided text. Aligns given text to the right.

Properties unique to image elements

The following properties are those unique to image elements:

Source

This isn't actually a property that can be adjusted through the Properties panel, but it does display the location of the imported image asset for reference.

Position

Contains settings for offsetting the image along both x and y positions.

Properties unique to symbol elements

The following properties are unique to symbol elements:

Playback Actions

These are not the same as actions that are defined within the **Actions** panel but are similar to primitive behaviors for **Symbol** instances. They allow us to influence the **Timeline** of the **Symbol** itself through commands placed upon the **Stage Timeline**.

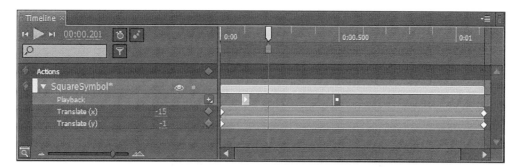

Scrub

This checkbox determines whether or not nested **Symbol Timeline** animations will follow along with **Stage Timeline** playback or not. This has no effect upon published compositions but exists only for convenience when authoring.

Properties available with the Stage

The Edge **Stage** itself also has a number of properties, which can be controlled through the **Properties** panel. In order to access the **Stage** properties, simply click anywhere on the **Stage** where another element is not present, or select the **Stage** **<div>** in the **Elements** panel.

Composition ID

A unique ID assigned to each Edge composition. This can be edited, but in most cases that is not necessary.

Document Title

This property sets the `<title>` tag value in the `<head>` of our HTML document.

Overflow

This property determines how the **Stage** behaves when elements extend past its borders. We have access to the same four choices as detailed above for rectangle elements.

Autoplay

Determines whether the composition should play immediately or wait for some command.

Background Color

The color to apply to our **Stage** background in RGBA format: Red, Green, Blue, Alpha.

> Unlike Flash (SWF) content, Edge animations can have semi-transparent background colors.

Width

This property sets the width of the **Stage**, in pixels.

Height

This property sets the height of the Stage, in pixels.

Color tools

These tools—**Background Color** and **Border Color**—allow us to quickly select the colors of a rectangle element before drawing it out upon the **Stage**.

Importing external assets

Aside from the creation of basic vector and text elements within an Edge composition, we also have the ability to import external assets for use in a project. These assets may have been prepared in another application such as Adobe Photoshop, Illustrator, or Fireworks. Generally, we would want to use these imported assets more than the simple shapes generated by Edge, but this will depend upon the project.

File types that can be imported into Edge include:

- SVG: Scalable Vector Graphics
- PNG: Portable Network Graphics
- JPEG: Joint Photographic Experts Group
- GIF: Graphics Interchange Format

We'll have a look at each of these formats and then go through a brief usage example.

 Files for this project are located in the ImportedAssets directory.

What is SVG?

Scalable Vector Graphics (SVG) is an XML-based file format that describes how to draw vector objects through polygon, path, and fill definitions. These objects are described in a way that informs SVG-capable clients of their structure and how everything should be visually rendered.

Working with Edge Tools and Managing Assets

SVG differs from bitmap formats such as JPG or PNG in that the image data is processed as needed, based upon the mathematical information contained within the SVG file. Because of this, these vector objects are easily scalable and can be represented at many different sizes with no apparent distortion while using the same base data.

In the following example, we see the SVG code for an object generated through Adobe Illustrator. This code is derived from the `star.svg` file, which is included in this book's assets. To view the vector object, simply drag this file into an SVG-capable browser and it will be rendered on-screen.

An excerpt of the file structure is as follows; if we want to view the entire structure, the file may be opened in a text editor such as Microsoft Notepad or Adobe Dreamweaver.

```
star.svg
<?xml version="1.0" encoding="utf-8"?>
<!-- Generator: Adobe Illustrator 15.1.0, SVG Export Plug-In . SVG
  Version: 6.00 Build 0)  -->

<!DOCTYPE svg PUBLIC "-//W3C//DTD SVG 1.1//EN"
  "http://www.w3.org/Graphics/SVG/1.1/DTD/svg11.dtd">
<svg version="1.1" id="Layer_1" xmlns="http://www.w3.org/2000/svg"
  xmlns:xlink="http://www.w3.org/1999/xlink" x="0px" y="0px"
  width="640px" height="480px" viewBox="0 0 640 480"
  enable-background="new 0 0 640 480" xml:space="preserve">
<g>
  <polygon fill="#414042" points="303,67.781 357.435,178.078
    479.153,195.764 391.076,281.617 411.869,402.845 303,345.609
    194.131,402.845 214.923,281.617 126.847,195.764 248.565,178.078
    "/>
  <g>
    <g>
      <polygon fill="none" points="263.211,48.892 219.32,137.825
        32.207,165.014 167.604,296.992 135.641,483.35 303,395.364
        470.36,483.35 438.396,296.992 573.793,165.014 386.68,137.825
        342.492,48.291 263.714,87.17 328.342,218.121 385.007,226.354
        344.003,266.322 353.683,322.76 303,296.114 252.316,322.76
        261.997,266.322 220.993,226.354 277.658,
        218.121 341.988,87.773
        "/>
```

```
<!--BULK OF SVG CODE REMOVED FOR BREVITY -->
      <path fill-rule="evenodd" clip-rule="evenodd"
         d="M84.896,167.553c0.984,0.127-2.648,0.475-1.372,0.811
         c-1.828-0.145-6.564,0.724-7.481,0.252c-4.083,0.807-6.354,
         1.543-3.53,2.104c-3.976,1.05-9.76,1.867-15.31,2.416c2.303,
         2.512,4.027,4.641,4.871,5.939c-0.943,1.146-5.629-1.
         925-11.134-6.977l-1.625-1.525c4.788-0.735,10.509-1.232,
         15.706-1.723c5.208-0.492,9.901-0.978,12.924-1.
         731c3.188-0.285,11.81-1.521,16.417-1.814c-0.303,0.429,0.396,
         0.217,1.244,0.547c-3.009,0.549-8.856,1.191-7.529,
         1.597C86.752,  167.576,85.693,167.61,84.896,167.553z"/>
    </g>
   </g>
  </g>
</svg>
```

Importing SVG images

To import a SVG file into Edge, we perform the following actions:

1. Navigate to the Edge application menu.
2. Select **File | Import...**
3. A system file browser dialog will appear. Navigate to the .svg file you wish to import.
4. Select the file and click **Open**.

5. The file will now be placed onto the **Stage** as shown in the following screenshot, and also added to the project **Library** under **Assets**. We can add multiple instances of this asset to the **Stage**.

 The file instance placed upon the **Stage** will be using the exact dimensions of the imported file itself, so it may overlap the boundaries of the **Stage**. This can be rectified through element manipulation by using the **Properties** panel. This is the same case in regard to bitmap images and is not unique to SVG.

What is a bitmap?

A bitmap is also referred to as a *Raster* image. Bitmap images are composed of a rectangular grid of individual pixels. Each pixel in this grid can include both color values and optionally transparency values (depending upon the image format).

Bitmap images are great for highly detailed images like photographs, since they define detail at a pixel level. They also do not require the client to perform any heavy calculations upon the image data in order to render it to a viewable state, as that information is already present within the pixel grid. The client simply has to read the data in properly.

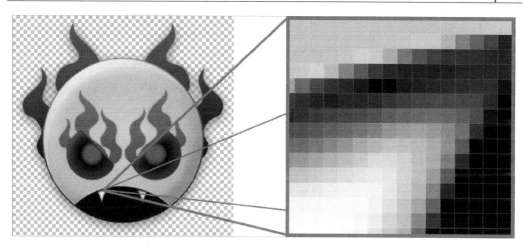

 Unlike SVG and other vector graphics formats, bitmap images are resolution-dependent, which means they cannot be scaled or otherwise manipulated without significant visual artifacting, causing the image to appear blurry or blocky.

Importing bitmap Images

To import a bitmap image file into Edge, we perform the following actions.

1. Navigate to the Edge application menu.
2. Select **File | Import…**
3. A system file browser dialog will appear. Navigate to the `.png`, `.gif`, or `.jpg` file you wish to import.
4. Select the file and click **Open**.

5. The file will now be placed onto the **Stage** as shown in the following screenshot and also added to the project **Library** under **Assets**. We can add multiple instances of this asset to the **Stage**.

 As with SVG files, the bitmap file instance placed upon the **Stage** will be using the exact dimensions of the imported file itself, so it may overlap the boundaries of the **Stage**. This can be remedied through element manipulation by using the **Properties** panel.

Working with imported assets

Any imported assets will always be available in the **Library** panel under **Assets**. From here, we can drag-and-drop instances onto the **Stage**.

 The **Assets** group within a project **Library** panel helps to keep thing organized and preserves imported files; even when all instances are removed from the **Stage**.

Converting assets into symbols

Symbols in Adobe Edge reside in the **Library** and are self-contained objects with their own **Timeline** and behaviors. Instances of **Symbols** can be dragged out of the **Library** and placed upon the main **Stage**, or even within other **Symbols**, where their properties can be adjusted like any other element.

 The **Autoplay timeline** option in this dialog determines whether the Symbol will play on its own or will require a manual command from the Edge API to begin playback.

Create a Symbol

To create a **Symbol** in Edge, perform the following steps.

1. Create a new Edge project and save it to the local disk.
2. Use the **Rectangle** tool to draw out an element upon the **Stage**.
3. If you wish, adjust the properties of your element before proceeding.
4. Be sure that your element is selected using the **Selection** tool.
5. In the Edge menu, choose **Modify | Convert to Symbol...**
6. A small **Create Symbol** dialog will appear which provides the option to give the **Symbol** a custom name. Type in a meaningful name and click **OK**.

The **Symbol** will now exist within the project **Library** and the original element will be converted into a **Symbol** instance on the **Stage**. To edit a **Symbol**, simply double-click it in the **Library**. Alternatively, double-click upon an instance of the **Symbol** upon the **Stage**. This will bring us into the **Symbol** itself for isolated editing.

Return to the main **Stage** by clicking upon the term **Stage** from within the edit mode.

The following screenshot depicts a created **Symbol**:

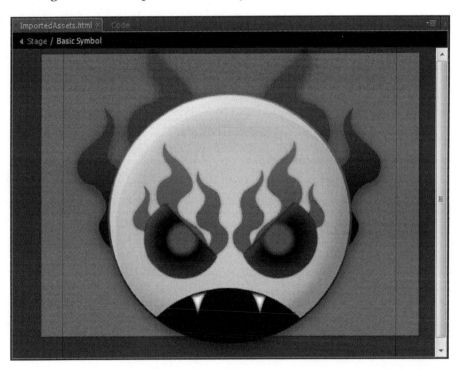

> Create many instances of the same **Symbol** by dragging them from the **Library** to the **Stage**. Adjusting properties of a **Symbol** instance will not change the original **Symbol** whatsoever.

Summary

In this chapter, we've examined how to use the drawing tools within Edge to add simple shapes and text areas to our composition. Additionally, we've had a look at importing assets created by other applications to be brought into an Edge project and used within a composition. Generally, no matter how each of these assets is created, they can all be employed within an Edge composition in very similar ways.

In the next chapter, we'll have a look at how to create motion through animating these elements along the Edge **Timeline**.

4
Creating Motion with Edge

The goal of Adobe Edge is to allow users to easily create standards-based motion and interaction without having to deal with a lot of code by hand. This chapter explores the motion side of the equation through animated content and the **Timeline**. We'll first examine the **Timeline** itself along with a variety of the controls that are built into this integral panel. We'll then move along through some demos in which we'll become familiar with both the **Playhead** and the **Mark**, along with a bit on element **Transitions**.

Animation within Edge

Similar to many digital animation programs, Edge employs the concept of "tweening" between keyframes. In traditional cell-based animation, a master animator would draw out certain key frames for an animation sequence and the frames in between these key frames would be created by apprentice or lower-ranked members of the animation team. The goal was always to create a smooth transition between each key frame created by the master animator, which would result in a completed animation sequence.

This process is performed programmatically within Edge. As keyframes are placed along the Timeline, Edge will fill in the time between with motion determined from the values gathered by adjacent keyframes. As authors, we have the additional ability to provide the tweening engine with instruction sets based upon a variety of easing equations. This allows a more natural flow between keyframes, and can also be used to achieve certain effects such as an elastic or bounce motion.

The Edge Timeline

The Timeline is where all of the motion in an Edge composition is orchestrated. The Timeline itself shares concepts and constructs from other Adobe applications, most notably Flash Professional and After Effects.

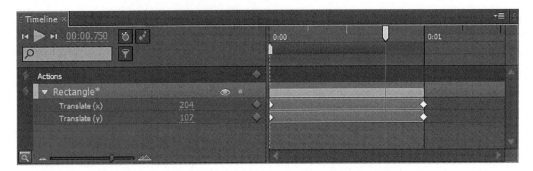

 Unlike the frame-based timeline in Flash Professional, the Edge Timeline is purely time-based.

Playback controls

The playback controls in Edge are all grouped together to in the upper left corner of the **Timeline** panel. These controls allow quick access to many of the playback options available through the **Timeline**.

Time

The time in Edge is measured in standard decimal timecode format: mm:ss.ddd, and this is how it is displayed in the **Time** control. As the **Playhead** moves along the **Timeline**, the information in this display is updated accordingly. A user can scrub the control to the left or right to adjust the current time, or simply click upon it, making it editable.

Search

The **Search** control appears as a small input box with a magnifying glass. This serves as a quick way to locate elements in the **Timeline** by element ID. It is very useful for larger projects with many animated elements.

Timeline options

These options can be toggled on or off depending upon your needs as they perform a variety of Timeline-related functions.

These options include the following:

- **Auto-Keyframe properties**: Selecting this option will enable Edge to generate keyframes for various properties automatically as they are adjusted along the Timeline. When not selected, any keyframes must be inserted manually.
- **Generate smooth transitions**: When selected, this informs Edge to use smooth transitions between element property adjustments as they are animated across time.
- **Only show animated elements**: When this option is selected, only those elements whose properties are animated will display within the Timeline. Static elements (such as a background image) will be hidden.

Timeline controls

There are basically only three controls within the Timeline that we need to be concerned with: the Playhead, the Mark, and a set of zoom controls. The functionality between controls varies greatly, as some are used for playback, some for animation, and others are simply there for convenience. All, however, are very useful.

The Playhead

The **Playhead** is the larger of the two elements on the **Timeline** and is represented by a solid red line, which indicates the current time. We can click upon the **Playhead** and scrub back and forth to change the current time. When an animation is being played back through Edge, the **Playhead** will move along with the current time.

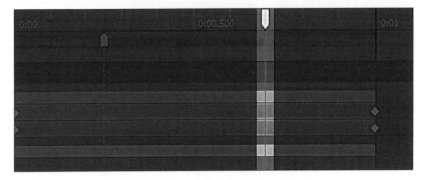

 Normally, the **Playhead** and the **Mark** are both synced. If not, they can be resynced through the application menu: **Timeline | Toggle Mark**.

The Mark

The **Mark** is a unique control to Edge. It is a way of pinning the current state of element properties to a certain time, while using the **Playhead** to determine at which time the animation should complete. The **Mark** can be positioned either before or after the time indicated by the **Playhead** — but it always indicates a starting point for the animation — with the **Playhead** indicating the end. Changing any element properties while the **Mark** is unsynced will create animation of those properties beginning at the **Mark** and ending at the **Playhead** position. In this way, we can quickly and freely create animation that is tightly controlled across the **Timeline**.

> To quickly sync or unsync the **Mark** from the **Playhead**, we can *Alt* + Click (Windows) or *Option* + Click (Mac) to toggle between each state.

Zoom controls

There are two zoom controls in Edge that allow us to expand and contract the Timeline. One is the **Zoom Timeline to Fit** button that appears as a small magnifying glass in the lower left corner of the **Timeline**. This will expand or contract the entire span of the visible **Timeline** to the current width of the **Timeline** panel. It can provide a good overview of the entire animation. The second control is a slider that appears directly to the right and allows the user to control the zoom level of the **Timeline** to accommodate whatever we are specifically trying to accomplish at any particular time.

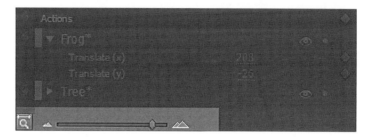

Keyframes

Similar to their representation in After Effects, keyframes in Edge appear along the Timeline as small diamonds. Unlike keyframes in Flash Professional, Edge keyframes are tied directly to the property that is being changed and not to the element itself. This allows for fine-grained property adjustments across the **Timeline** for any particular element. It is very flexible and a powerful way to animate selected element properties.

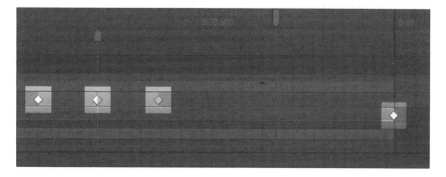

Creating motion

Animating element properties within Edge is fairly straightforward. In this section, we're going to step through a number of basic ways to animate elements along the Edge Timeline, once using only the **Playhead**, and again using the **Playhead** in conjunction with the **Mark**. By performing the same animation in each way, we will get a feel for the different workflow styles that Edge makes available to us when animating element properties across time.

Animating with the Playhead

We will now do a simple animation of an element moving from one side of the Stage to the other, while rotating and changing color using the Playhead along with the Properties panel.

1. Create a new Edge project and save it to your local disk.

   Adjust the **Stage** as follows by using the **Properties** panel:
   - **Stage W**: 600 px
   - **Stage H**: 350 px
   - **Background Color**: #000000
   - **Overflow**: hidden

2. Using the **Rectangle** tool, draw out an element upon the **Stage**. We will modify its properties in the next step, so do not worry about dimensions or shape.

3. For each property listed below, make the following adjustments within the **Properties** panel:
   - **Location X**: 20 px
   - **Location Y**: 230 px
   - **Size W**: 100 px
   - **Size H**: 100 px
   - **Background Color**: #c0c0c0

4. Still using the **Properties** panel, click upon the **Keyframe** diamond next to the properties for **Location**, **Background Color**, and **Rotation**. This will set a keyframe for each property within the **Timeline**.

5. Be sure that **Auto-Keyframe Properties** is selected in the **Timeline**. As we have already marked each of these properties with initial keyframes, any adjustments we make across time will be auto-keyframed.

Chapter 4

6. Our project should now appear as shown in the following screenshot. We are now ready to proceed with the remainder of this exercise.

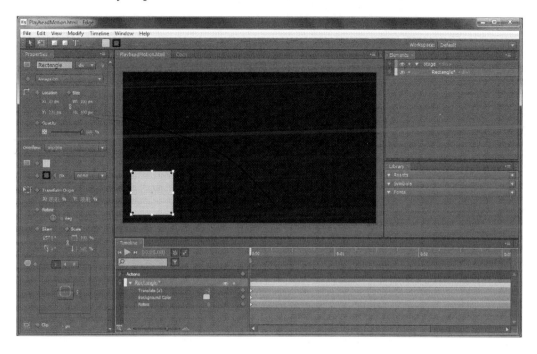

7. Drag the **Playhead** over to the ruler marker labeled `0:04` and release.
8. Now, select the element with the **Selection** tool and in the **Properties** panel, modify the following properties:
    - **Location X**: `480 px`
    - **Background Color**: `#900000`
    - **Rotation**: `480 deg`

   Notice that we now have transition bars appear on the **Timeline** with another set of keyframes at the end of our animation sequence.

9. We can now either scrub through the **Timeline** by dragging the **Playhead** back and forth, or hit the **Play** button to view the full sequence.

Creating Motion with Edge

When played back, the element should appear to roll along the **Stage** from left to right, changing from gray to red as it does so. The resulting end state is displayed in following screenshot:

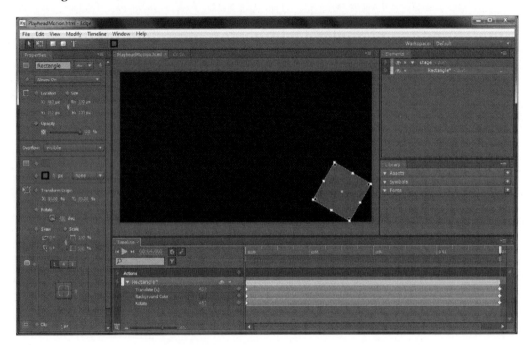

 Note that any of the properties of an element can be keyframed, and thus modified over time in the way we have done.

Animating with the Mark

Now we will perform the preceding exercise, but this time will employ the **Mark** to demonstrate an alternative way of creating motion in Edge.

1. Create a new Edge project and save it to your local disk.
2. Adjust the **Stage** as follows by using the **Properties** panel:
    - **Stage W**: 600 px
    - **Stage H**: 350 px
    - **Background Color**: #000000
    - **Overflow**: hidden

3. Using the **Rectangle** tool, draw out an element upon the **Stage**. We will modify its properties in the next step, so do not worry about dimensions or shape.

4. For each property listed, make the following adjustments within the **Properties** panel:
   - **Location** X: 20 px
   - **Location** Y: 230 px
   - **Size W**: 100 px
   - **Size H**: 100 px
   - **Background Color**: #c0c0c0

5. Drag the **Playhead** to 0:04 in the **Timeline**.

6. Now, go to the application menu and select **Timeline | Toggle Mark**. This will unsync the **Mark** from the **Playhead**. Again, the **Mark** is the small control directly beneath the **Playhead** when unsynced.

7. Grab the **Mark** and drag it to 0:00 in the **Timeline**. This will pin the element's current properties to the 0:00 point without the need to manually insert keyframes. Keep the **Playhead** itself at 0:04.

8. Now select the element with the **Selection** tool, and in the **Properties** panel modify the following properties:
   - **Location X**: 480 px
   - **Background Color**: #900000
   - **Rotation**: 480 deg

9. Notice that we now have transition bars appear on the **Timeline** without the need to set any keyframes whatsoever.

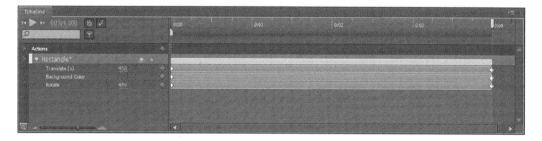

Creating Motion with Edge

10. Go to the application menu and select **Timeline | Toggle Mark** to sync the **Mark**. We can also toggle the **Mark** through a keyboard shortcut as expressed earlier in this chapter.

11. We can now either scrub through the **Timeline** by dragging the **Playhead** back and forth, or hit the **Play** button to view the full sequence.

When played back, the element should appear to roll along the **Stage** from left to right, changing from gray to red as it does so.

In the example shown, the **Mark** was placed at an earlier time in relation to the **Playhead** within our **Timeline**, which need not be the case. We can also place the **Mark** at a later time than the **Playhead** and the same behavior will be exhibited: current properties are pinned to the **Mark** position while adjusted properties align to the position of the **Playhead**.

Editing Transition

You may have noticed that the motion achieved through the examples presented so far have been plain, linear transitions from one value to another. To provide a greater sense of realism and a fuller, dynamic nature to individual transitions, we also have the ability to assign a variety of **Easing** equations to our transitions.

Note that when changing the easing behavior of a transition, we can select the entire element transition, or we may choose individual property transitions to apply a variety of transition types to the same element. It is quite flexible.

Duration

This value represents the time taken up by the entire transition. Transitions can be extended or shortened easily through the use of this control. Modification of this value will impact the **End** value of the transition, but has no effect upon transition **Delay**.

Delay

Determines when the transition should begin, measured from the start of the overall **Timeline**. Modification of this value will shift the transition start time but has no effect upon **Duration**.

End

This time value marks the end of a particular transition within the **Timeline**. Modifying the **End** value through this control will effectively extend the duration of the transition.

Easing

There are many easing choices within Adobe Edge. The default is **linear**, which will simply express a transition from A to B in an entirely linear fashion. Often, an easing algorithm of a more dynamic nature is required to express a bit more realism in motion, or to achieve a specific effect. Edge comes bundled with no less than 29 easing choices to provide the user with a variety of options when determining transition easing.

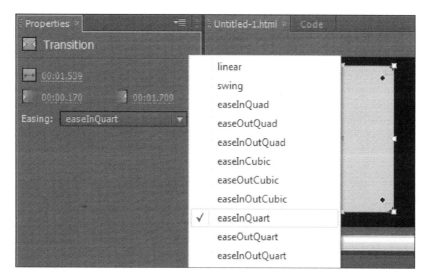

> The transition-easing algorithms available in Edge are similar to others found in many ActionScript libraries for animating Flash content. Unlike in Flash Professional, Edge does not yet have the ability to customize these presets.

Example: Animating a website header

One of the basic use cases for Edge is the creation of a simply animated website header. We will be authoring such a composition for a studio recording project of the name *An Early Morning Letter, Displaced* who wish to have images of each of their releases animate on the header itself. Thankfully, they have provided us with all of the assets necessary for the construction of this animated header.

> These assets are included as part of the files for this chapter and are in the folder named `banner_assets`.

Project setup, asset import, and general layout

The first step in this composition will be to set up our Edge project, import all of the assets, and arrange them upon the **Stage**. We will begin by arranging the assets in their final form, as they should appear at the end of the animation once it has completed playback. The **Mark** makes it quite easy to animate backwards.

1. Create a new Edge project and save it onto the local disk.

   Adjust the **Stage** as follows by using the **Properties** panel:
   - **Stage W**: `940 px`
   - **Stage H**: `198 px`
   - **Background Color**: `#000000`
   - **Overflow**: `hidden`

2. Go to the application menu and select **File | Import...** to bring up a file browser.

3. Select all of the `.png` files located within the provided assets folder and click **Open**. The selected files will be placed upon the **Stage** and also added to the project **Library**.

4. The background image is the exact size of the **Stage** itself and should fill this entire area.

5. The album art can be arranged evenly across the bottom of the **Stage** as seen in the following screenshot. We can use the mouse or the **Properties** panel to arrange these images. Space them evenly apart from one another.

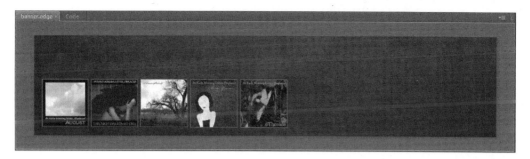

6. Finally, we need to add a title to this header animation. We'll use the **Text** tool to form the project's name along the top of the header. Choose the **Text** tool now.

7. Add a new text element to the **Stage** and type the term `An Early Morning Letter, Displaced` into the field.

8. With this text element selected, enter the **Properties** panel and make the following adjustments:
    - **Location X**: `16 px`
    - **Location Y**: `11 px`
    - **Font Name**: `Arial Black, Gadget, sans-serif`
    - **Font Size**: `40 px`
    - **Font Color**: `#bbbbbb`

9. We should now have a composition that appears as shown in the following screenshot:

Creating Motion with Edge

Animating elements

We will now perform the animation of all elements on the **Stage** through use of the **Playhead**, **Mark**, and **Properties** panel.

Animating the background

We will create a transition lasting `00:07.000`, which will fade in the background element while slightly adjusting its scale.

1. Using the **Selection** tool, click on the **bg** element to bring up its properties.
2. In the **Timeline**, move the **Mark** to `00:07.000` and the **Playhead** to `00:00.000`.
3. Using the **Properties** panel, make the following adjustments:
    - **Scale** (linked): `115 %`
    - **Opacity**: `25 %`
4. In the **Timeline**, click upon the transition that we have just created to select it.
5. In the **Properties** panel, change the **Easing** selection to `easeOutSine` to determine how the transition should occur upon playback. Leave the scale transitions as `linear`.

Animating the cover art (do this for each cover art image)

For each image, we will create a transition lasting `00:02.000`, which will slide the image in from off-screen, resulting in a playful bounce before coming to a rest. We will stagger the transitions of each subsequent image to begin at the midpoint of the previous transition, creating a flurry motion within the composition.

1. Using the **Selection** tool, click on the **fvm001** element to bring up its properties.
2. In the **Timeline**, move the **Mark** to `00:02.090` and the **Playhead** to `00:00.000`.
3. Using the **Properties** panel, make the following adjustment:
    - **Location X**: `986 px`
4. In the **Timeline**, click upon the opacity transition that we have just created to select it.
5. In the **Properties** panel, change the **Easing** selection to `easeOutBounce` to determine how the transition should occur upon playback.
6. Repeat the previous steps for each of the other album art images.

Chapter 4

 Edge also includes the option to paste various elements of a transition from one object to another. For repeatable transitions such as this one, we may want to have a look at the **Paste Special** commands under the application **Edit** menu.

Animating the title text

We will create a transition lasting `00:05.500`, which will fade in the title text element.

1. Using the **Selection** tool, click on the `Title` element to bring up its properties.
2. In the **Timeline**, move the **Mark** to `00:06.000` and the **Playhead** to `00:05.000`.
3. Using the **Properties** panel, make the following adjustment:
    - **Opacity:** `0 %`
4. In the **Timeline**, click upon the transition that we have just created to select it.
5. In the **Properties** panel, change the **Easing** selection to `easeInCubic` to determine how the transition should occur upon playback.

Once all of the elements are added to the **Stage**, positioned correctly, and animated properly through transitions, the Edge **Timeline** will look similar to what we see in the following screenshot.

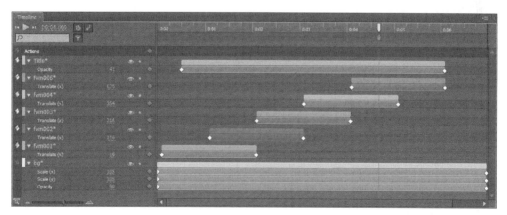

 Edge makes it easy to see exactly what is going on in a composition through fine-grained transition indicators which correspond to individual element properties.

[93]

The result of our animated banner appears in a web browser, as shown in the following screenshot. To publish an Edge composition to the browser, we can choose **File | Preview in Browser** from the application menu.

 Notice that there is no interactivity with any of the elements in this banner. In the next chapter, we'll wire up a number of ways to interact with individual elements within this composition.

Summary

In this chapter, we've examined how to create motion in Adobe Edge by making use of the **Timeline, Playhead, Mark,** and **Properties** panel. Those who are familiar with Flash Professional or After Effects should recognize just how familiar many of these concepts are, and possibly how refined and evolved these concepts have become as implemented in the Edge application interface. It is quite easy to both create and edit animation within an Edge composition!

In this next chapter, we'll have a look at how to add interactivity to an Edge project through the use of **Actions** and **Triggers**.

5
Adding Interactivity to an Edge Composition

The Adobe Edge Runtime API allows us to easily add basic interactivity to our compositions in the form of mouse interactions, touch interactions, and some core timeline and playback behaviors. This is all accomplished through the **Actions** panel and the small pieces of JavaScript code available to us to make changes depending upon what we are trying to accomplish with any given element.

In this chapter, we will have a look at the various types of actions and triggers that we can apply to an Edge project. We'll also have a look at adding interactivity to our sample web banner from the previous chapter, and will consider the Edge Runtime APIs before moving on.

Working with Actions

Actions are the primary way of creating interactivity within Adobe Edge. They can be applied to either a single element, the entire **Stage**, or through certain points along the **Timeline** as triggers. The code utilized through the **Actions** panel is all JavaScript and relies on two JavaScript libraries: jQuery, and the Adobe Edge Runtime.

Adding Interactivity to an Edge Composition

 Unlike with Adobe Flash Professional, code can be applied to any element, which means the elements do not have to be created as symbols to receive actions upon them.

There are many types of actions that can be applied to a project depending upon the element receiving the interaction, but they generally involve either playback instructions or element reference and manipulation.

The Timeline Actions layer

The Edge Timeline includes a special layer set apart from all the others that is called the **Actions** layer and is used explicitly for plotting special actions, called Triggers, at various points along the **Timeline**.

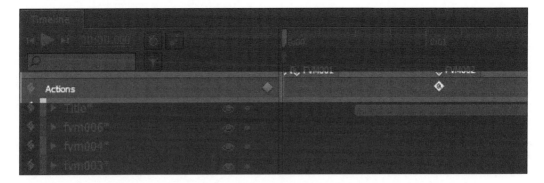

 For many years, when working in Flash Professional, it has been the recommended practice to create a specialized layer labeled "Actions" within which any timeline ActionScript is included. Edge borrows this long-established workflow practice to great effect.

Working with Triggers

Triggers can be created along the **Timeline** in a number of ways. The most direct method is to place the **Playhead** at a point in which we want to include a trigger and then use the keyboard shortcut *Ctrl+t* (Windows) or *Cmd+t* (Mac). Alternatively, we can either click the keyframe diamond in the **Actions** layer or go to the application menu and choose **Timeline | Insert Trigger**.

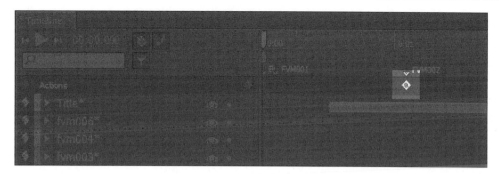

To edit an existing trigger, simply double-click it and the **Actions** panel will pop up, allowing us to make any adjustments. Triggers can also be dragged to any time along the **Timeline** using the mouse.

Working with Labels

Labels in Edge are a mechanism by which we are able to set textual markers along the Timeline. These markers are able to provide visual authoring cues or can be referenced through **Actions**. For instance, if we were to set a Label named `JumpPoint` at `0:02.000`, we could then reference it as follows:

```
sym.play("JumpPoint");
```

in place of:

```
sym.play(2000);
```

 Those working in Flash Professional will recognize the concept of working with Labels. In the application Flash Professional, they are known as "frame labels" and can be used in the exact same way.

Applying Actions to the Stage

As the Stage itself is, in fact, a Symbol, it should come as no surprise that actions can be assigned directly to the Stage. To assign a new action to the Stage, select the Stage by deselecting all other elements within the **Edge** composition, and access the **Properties** panel. Click upon the script icon to open the **Actions** panel to configure a set of actions for the **Stage**.

 Alternatively, Stage actions can be set through the **Elements** panel in the same manner.

The Stage, due to its unique nature, can have some unique actions applied to it as listed in the following:

- **compositionReady**: These instructions will fire immediately once the composition is loaded
- **scroll**: Used so we are able to scroll the contents of the Stage
- **keydown**: Keyboard detection of key-down events
- **keyup**: Keyboard detection of key-up events

For instance, to detect when the user hits the space bar, place the following code upon a **keydown** action:

```
// e.which tells you which key. e.g. 32 = space
if (e.which == 32) {
   // do something
}
```

The following short list gives some of the more common key codes that can be used through JavaScript. Full charts can be found online if so desired.

- 13 = enter
- 16 = shift
- 17 = control
- 18 = alt
- 32 = space
- 37 = left
- 38 = up
- 40 = down
- 49 = right

Applying Actions to individual elements

For many actions, such as **mouse clicks**, **hover effects**, and things of that nature, we will want to apply code directly to certain elements. The quickest way to do this is to go to the **Elements** panel and click upon the small script icon next to the desired element. This will open the **Actions** panel within which we can specify an appropriate action.

A common example of an individual element action would be a click event within which we direct the **Playhead** to play from position `1000` along the **Timeline**.

```
// play the timeline from the given position (ms or label)
sym.play(1000);
```

Adding Interactivity to an Edge Composition

Overview: The Adobe Edge Runtime APIs

Edge compositions are dependent upon the inclusion of both jQuery and Edge Runtime JavaScript libraries in order to animate elements and provide interactivity.

For these examples, we will be looking at the raw code within the project {name}_edgeActions.js file after applying the said actions. This file is arranged as follows:

```
/
* Adobe Edge Composition Actions
* Edit this file with caution, being careful to preserve
* function signatures and comments starting with 'Edge' to maintain
* the ability to interact with these actions from within Adobe Edge
/
(function($, Edge, compId){
  var Composition = Edge.Composition, Symbol = Edge.Symbol;
  // aliases for commonly used Edge classes
  //Edge symbol: 'stage'
  (function(symbolName) {
    Symbol.bindElementAction(compId, symbolName, "${_fvm001}",
      "mouseover", function(sym, e) {
      // Change an Element's contents.
      //   (sym.$("name") resolves an Edge element name to a DOM
      //   element that can be used with jQuery)
      sym.$("Info").html("August (2000)");
    });

    //Edge binding end
    /*
    REDUNDANT FUNCTIONAL CONTENT REMOVED FOR THIS EXAMPLE...
    */
  })("stage");
  //Edge symbol end:'stage'
})(jQuery, AdobeEdge, "EDGE-5392063514");
```

Document Object Model events

Document Object Model (DOM) events are tied to the Edge composition Stage. These events fire when the composition is ready, when scrolling occurs, or when the keyboard is interacted with through keydown or keyup actions.

Example:

```
Symbol.bindElementAction(compId, symbolName, "document",
  "compositionReady", function(sym, e) {
  sym.play();
  // insert code for compositionReady event here
});
//Edge binding end
```

 Read up on the DOM at: http://www.w3.org/DOM/

Mouse events

These are normal mouse events that are registered upon individual Edge elements. Use these when targeting when a user presses or releases the mouse button, among other things.

Example:

```
Symbol.bindElementAction(compId, symbolName, "${_Rectangle}",
  "mousedown", function(sym, e) {
  // stop the timeline at the given position (ms or label)
  sym.stop(1000);
  // insert code for mousedown here
});
//Edge binding end
```

 Generally, these actions can be applied to the Stage as well.

Touch events

Touch events are to be used when targeting touch-enabled devices such as smartphones and tablets; we can detect when a touch begins, touch movements, and touch-end events to perform certain functions within an Edge composition.

Example:

```
Symbol.bindElementAction(compId, symbolName, "${_Rectangle}",
  "touchstart", function(sym, e) {
  // Navigate to a new URL in the current window
  // (replace "_self" with another name for a new window)
  window.open("http://www.adobe.com", "_self");
  // insert code for touchstart here
});
//Edge binding end
```

> Similarly to mouse events, these actions can also be applied to the Stage or individual elements.

Virtual mouse events

Virtual mouse events are interesting. The jQuery Mobile library, which the Edge Runtime references, includes the concept of virtual mice that can function as mouse events in a desktop environment but act as touch events on mobile devices.

Example:

```
Symbol.bindElementAction(compId, symbolName, "${_Rectangle}",
  "vmousedown", function(sym, e) {
  sym.playReverse();
  // insert code for vmousedown here
});
//Edge binding end
```

> Read up on the jQuery Mobile virtual mouse events: http://jquerymobile.com/test/docs/api/events.html

Timeline events

Timeline events allow you to control the Edge composition timeline. Examples include `update`, `play`, `complete`, and `stop`.

Example:

```
sym.play();
```

> Many of these actions, such as **Go To** and **Stop** have close counterparts in the world of Flash and ActionScript.

Adobe is developing an online reference to the Edge Runtime, which can be accessed from the following URL:

`http://labs.adobe.com/technologies/edge/resources/jsapi.html`

The following screenshot is of the URL page:

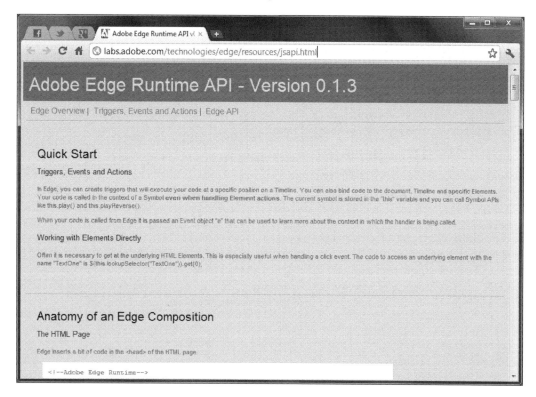

Example: Adding interactivity to a website header

Now that we've had a solid overview of how to apply interactivity through **Actions** within an Edge composition, let's revisit our example project from the previous chapter. If you recall, we have created an animated website header for a studio recording project of the name An Early Morning Letter, Displaced.

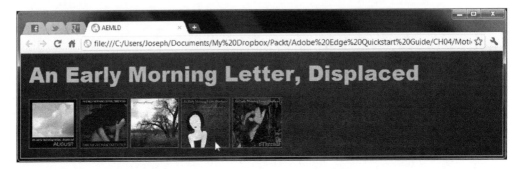

They like what we've done with the composition so far but now request that we make it a bit more interactive. Specifically, they want a hover effect where rolling over each piece of album art brings up some basic information about that release. Additionally, they would like to have their website open when a user clicks upon the title text and direct links to each album page when the album art is clicked.

Creating the Text element

First we must open the project and create a new text element on the **Stage** to contain the hover text, which they wish to display.

1. Open the website header project from the previous chapter. If desired, a completed version of that project can be located within the `MotionBanner` folder.

2. Save this project to a new location, so that if we make a disastrous mistake, the original project is not lost. Note that it is always important to version or back up our files in an organized fashion.

3. Using the **Text** tool, drag a new text element out onto the **Stage**.

4. Upon releasing the mouse button, the **Selection** tool will activate automatically with the new **Text** element selected. We will want to leave the text element empty for now.

5. Within the **Properties** panel, make the following adjustments:

   ID: `Info`

   Location:
   - **X**: `530 px`
   - **Y**: `83 px`

   Size:
   - **W**: `392 px`
   - **H**: `96 px`

   Font Name: `Arial Black, Gadget, sans-serif`

   Font Size: `18 px`

   Font Color: `#808080`

The text element is now set up properly.

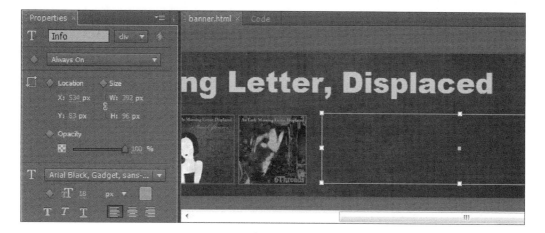

 As the text element actually contains no text at this point, when unselected, we may have a difficult time locating it for any further manipulation. This is not a problem; simply click it in the **Elements** panel to select it once again.

Adding interactivity to the Title

We will need to add a **click** action to the **Title** element, allowing a user to click off into the artist's website. To do so, we perform the following steps:

1. Within the **Elements** panel, click the script icon next to the **Title** element. This will bring up the **Actions** panel.
2. We are immediately presented with a number of actions to choose from. Select the **click** action.
3. From the right column, select **Open URL**. Some code along with comments is inserted into the editor.
4. Change the code, so that it appears to read as follows:

   ```
   window.open("http://displaced.memoryspiral.com/", "_self");
   ```

This portion of the example is now complete and can be seen in the following screenshot:

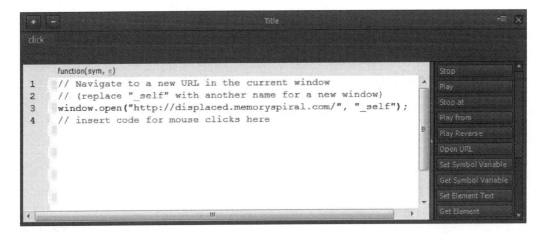

Adding interactivity to the album art

There are three separate actions that we need to assign to each of the album images in this composition; **click**, **mouseover**, and **mouseout**. We will repeat the following steps for each element, changing the necessary parameters as needed.

1. Within the **Elements** panel, click the script icon next to one of the album art image elements. For this example, we'll choose the `fvm004` element. This will bring up the **Actions** panel.
2. We are immediately presented with a number of actions to choose from. Select the **click** action.

3. From the right column, select **Open URL**. Some codes along with comments are inserted into the editor.

4. Change the code that appears to read as follows:
   ```
   window.open("http://fracturedvisionmedia.com/FVM004/", "_self");
   ```

5. We need to select two more actions to choose from. First, we click the little + icon at the top of the **Actions** panel and select the **mouseover** action.

6. From the right column, select **Set Element Text**. Some codes along with comments are inserted into the editor.

7. Change the code that appears to read as follows:
   ```
   sym.$("Info").html("Shudderflowers (2009)");
   ```

8. This will change our dynamic text element to display information regarding this album.

> Notice that we are changing text within the Info text element that was previously created. Element IDs are important not only for our own recognition, but are also used to target specific elements in cases as shown.

9. For the final action, we will click the little + icon at the top of the **Actions** panel and select the **mouseout** action.

10. From the right column, select **Set Element Text** just as before. Code will be inserted to the editor.

11. Change the code that appears to read as follows:
    ```
    sym.$("Info").html("");
    ```
    This will clear out any of the text inserted through our **mouseover** command.

We have now enabled three separate actions upon this element: a **click**, to open more details in the web browser, a **mouseover**, to display some general text to the user upon hover, and **mouseout** to remove the text when the cursor is no longer present over the element.

We have demonstrated how to accomplish this for one of the five album image elements. To complete the exercise, we will need to repeat this for each element. A completed example of this project can be found in the `InteractiveBanner` folder.

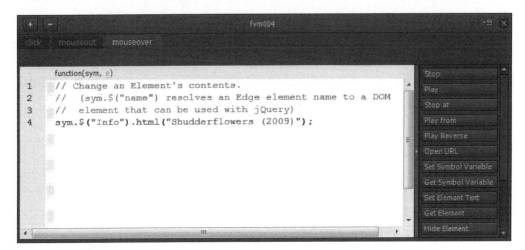

 If desired, entire sets of actions can be copied from one element to be pasted within another. To accomplish this, use the **Selection** tool and select the element containing the desired actions. Copy the element through the application menu: **Edit | Copy**. Now select the element to receive the actions and return to the application menu: **Edit | Paste Special | Paste Actions**. Now we can simply open the **Actions** panel and tweak the pasted actions as desired.

Completing the final website header composition

We are now ready to produce the final files for our client. To publish our Edge composition to the browser, we can choose **File | Preview in Browser** from the application menu. This will write all necessary files and open the completed composition in a web browser.

Now that we have added interactivity to this banner, we can hover over each image to get more information about it. Clicking upon the image will open details within the browser. Clicking upon the title will also open a website.

 The examples shown are some types of interactivity that can be achieved through Edge. We can have a look at the Edge Runtime API and documentation for more examples.

Summary

In this chapter, we've examined how to use the **Actions** panel to add interactivity to an Edge composition through element actions and timeline triggers. Edge uses JavaScript as its scripting language through the Edge Runtime APIs due to its adherence to web standards. Those familiar with ActionScript versions 1 or 2 from Flash Professional should feel quite at home, as will anyone coming from another JavaScript-based coding environment.

In the final chapter of this book, we'll have a look at some other resources to help you get the most out of Adobe Edge.

6
Additional Resources

In this Quickstart Guide, we've just scratched the surface of Adobe Edge. There are many resources available online for you to delve deeper into the application, and Packt Publishing has a book scheduled for mid-2012, which will explore much more of Adobe Edge in its final form, tentatively titled *"Learning Adobe Edge"*.

In this chapter, we present some information on integrating Edge content into an existing website, followed by a listing of other resources, which will assist the reader in exploring all that the Adobe Edge application has to offer. Finally, we'll have a look at an overview of the forthcoming *Learning Adobe Edge* book.

Using an Edge composition within an existing website

While some Edge compositions make sense on their own, we will generally want to integrate content produced with Edge into an existing website.

We'll need to include everything in the Adobe Edge Runtime code block. This includes moving this entire code block into another HTML document's `<head>` area, moving all of the actual files into the existing website directory structure, and then updating any references that may have changed.

```html
<!--Adobe Edge Runtime-->
  <script type="text/javascript" charset="utf-8"
    src="banner_edgePreload.js"></script>
<!--Adobe Edge Runtime End-->
```

Additional Resources

We'll also need to copy and paste the Stage itself into our existing document. This is the easy bit; simply copy and paste this `<div>` into the document `<body>` and then position as desired through CSS.

```
<div id="stage" class="EDGE-5392063514"></div>
```

Online resources

While Adobe Edge is still a very new application (especially considering that it is still in preview status), there are still a number of useful resources available for those just starting out with this technology.

The following are a variety of other resources for learning Edge:

- **Adobe Edge Preview**:

    http://labs.adobe.com/technologies/edge/

    For downloads, FAQs, sample projects

- **Adobe Edge Community Forums**:

    http://forums.adobe.com/community/labs/edge/

    The official Adobe Edge public discussion forums

- **Adobe Edge Runtime APIs**:

    http://labs.adobe.com/technologies/edge/resources/jsapi.html

    The Adobe Edge developer documentation

- **@AdobeEdge**:

    http://twitter.com/adobeedge

    The only official Adobe Edge Twitter account

- **Adobe Edge Wikipedia Article**:

    http://en.wikipedia.org/wiki/Adobe_Edge

- **Edge Kingdom**:

    http://www.edgekingdom.com/

    A third-party resource

- **Adobe Edge Forum**:

    http://www.adobe-edge-forum.com/

    A third-party resource

Look out for the full version of Adobe Edge, to be released soon! Meanwhile, Adobe does plan on making available milestone builds as public previews, which can be obtained from Adobe Labs: http://labs.adobe.com/technologies/edge/.

About the forthcoming book: Learning Adobe Edge

This book enables even those with little knowledge of HTML or programming web content to freely create a variety of rich compositions involving motion and interactivity. Detailed within is everything you need to know to effectively use the Adobe Edge application.

 Book title and cover subject to change.

Learning Adobe Edge

Robust motion and interactivity through web standards

The book will take you through the following:

- Learn to use Adobe's newest Creative Suite application to create engaging motion and rich interactivity
- Master the Edge interface and unleash your creativity through standard HTML, CSS, and JavaScript
- Packed with an abundance of information regarding the Edge application and related toolsets
- Those approaching Edge from Adobe Flash Professional will find many references and tips for a smooth transition
- A comprehensive beginner's guide for creating engaging content with Adobe Edge

Learning Adobe Edge will detail how to use this professional authoring software to create highly engaging content that targets HTML5, CSS, and JavaScript. Content created in Adobe Edge does not rely on a plugin, so it can be run within any standard browser, even on a mobile.

We'll provide the reader with a full overview of the current web landscape, shifting toward an overview of the Edge application itself. From here, we will move on to look at the various panels and toolsets available, and explore the many options we have when creating motion and interactivity using Edge.

The book presents the reasoning behind creating engaging, standards-based web content, and how Edge fills the need for professional tooling in this area. We'll examine content creation, the importing of external assets, how to achieve fluid animation and advanced transitioning through the Edge timeline, Interactivity through Actions and Triggers, and workflow options across Adobe Creative Suite applications. Sprinkled throughout the book are tips and references for those coming to Edge from a background in Flash Professional. Towards the end of the book, the reader will explore a variety of more advanced topics such as the Edge Runtime APIs and how Edge can interface with other Creative Suite applications for a full workflow. Whether the reader is coming to Edge from Flash Professional or is totally new to motion graphics on the web, *Learning Adobe Edge* will provide a solid foundation of motion and interactivity concepts and techniques along with a set of demo assets to build upon. In the end, you'll have a firm grasp of what it takes to create engaging content for the web and the familiarity with Edge to actually get it done!

Additional Resources

What you will learn

- Gain an understanding of the shifting web landscape
- Effectively compare Adobe Edge to Adobe Flash Professional motion tools
- Become familiar with all elements of the Edge application interface
- Use the drawing tools in Edge to create and manipulate elements on the Stage
- Import rich graphics for use in Adobe Edge compositions
- Animate a range of elements with full transitioning through Timeline keyframes
- Employ JavaScript to add interactivity to your project through Actions and Triggers
- Author a range of expressive compositions using nothing but web standards
- Become familiar with the Adobe Edge Runtime APIs for deep manipulation of on-screen elements
- Employ other Adobe Creative Suite tools in your workflow to get the most out of Edge

If you are interested in creating engaging motion-and-interactive compositions using web standards with professional tooling, then this book is for you. Using this book, you can get started with creating animation and highly interactive projects that run in any web browser, even on mobile devices!

Index

Symbols

@AdobeEdge 113
.edge file type 13
.html file 14
+ icon 107

A

Actions
　about 95, 96
　applying, to individual elements 99
　applying, to Stage 98
　labels, working with 97
　Timeline Actions layer 96
　triggers, working with 96
actions panel 48
Adobe
　Edge tool 5
Adobe AIR 12
Adobe Edge
　Adobe Edge Runtime 13, 16
　animation 79
　application interface overview 25
　comparing with, Adobe Flash Professional 7-9
　CSS 14
　file types, importing 69
　goal 79
　history 12, 13
　HTML 14
　installing 16, 17
　interactive contents 12
　interface overview 25
　JavaScript 14, 15
　jQuery 13
　jQuery, using 15
　menu system 29
　need for 5, 6
　online resources 112
　panels 44
　Stage 42
　symbols 75
　using 11
　using, within website 111
　web animation 12
　welcome screen 18, 19
　working 13
Adobe Edge Community Forums 113
Adobe Edge Forum 113
Adobe Edge Preview 112
Adobe Edge Runtime 16
Adobe Edge Runtime API 95
Adobe Edge Runtime APIs
　about 113
　DOM events 101
　mouse events 101
　overview 100
　timeline events 103
　touch events 102
Adobe Edge Wikipedia Article 113
Adobe Flash Professional
　about 7-9
　actions 9
　keyframes 8
　library 9
　stage 7
　symbols 8
　timeline 8
Align Center property 67
Align Left property 67
Align Right property 67

Alt + Click 83
animation
  about 79
  creating 84
  Mark, using 86, 88
  Playhead, using 84, 85
  Transition, editing 88
  website header, animating 90
application interface
  Edge panel layout, customizing 26, 27
  overview 25
  window 26
  workspaces, creating 28, 29
  workspaces, managing 27
Assets group 75
Autoplay property 68

B

Background Color property 65, 68
bitmap
  about 72
  images, importing 73, 74
Bold property 66
Border Color property 65
Border Radius property 66
Border Thickness property 66

C

Cascading Style Sheets. *See* **CSS**
Clip property 65
color tools 69
Composition ID property 68
CSS 14

D

Document Object Model. *See* **DOM**
Document Title property 68
DOM 101
drawing tools
  about 51, 52
  Rectangle tool 52
  Rounded Rectangle tool 53
  Selection tool 62
  Text tool 56
  Transform tool 62

E

Edge Kingdom 113
Edge Timeline
  about 44, 80
  playback controls 80
Edge Toolbar
  about 36
  Background Color 42
  Border Color 42
  Rectangle tool 39
  Rounded Rectangle tool 40
  Selection tool 37
  Text tool 41
  Transform tool 38
edit options
  Copy 31
  Cut 31
  Delete 31
  Duplicate 31
  Paste 31
  Paste Special 31
  Redo 31
  Select All 31
  Undo 31
element animation
  background, animating 92
  cover art, animating 92
  title text, animating 93, 94
Element Display property 64
Elements panel 45, 98
element types, properties
  Clip 65
  Element Display 64
  ID 64
  Location 64
  opacity 64
  Rotate 65
  Scale 65
  size 64
  Skew 65
  Tag 64
  Transform Origin 64

F

file options
  Close 30

Close All 30
Exit 30
Import 30
New 30
Open 30
Open Recent 30
Preview In Browser 30
Revert 30
Save 30
Save As... 30
file types, importing into Adobe Edge
  GIF 69
  imported assets, working 75
  JPEG 69
  PNG 69
  SVG 69
Font Name property 66
Font Size property 66
Font Size Units property 66

G

General Layout 90, 91

H

Height property 69
Help option
  About Adobe Edge.. 36
  About JavaScript API.. 36
  About Product Improvement Program .. 36
HTML
  <audio> tag 10
  <canvas> tag 10
  <video> tag 10
  about 10, 14
Hyper Text Markup Language. *See* **HTML**

I

image elements, properties
  Position 67
  Source 67
installing
  Adobe Edge 16, 17
interactivity
  adding, to album art 106-108
  adding, to title 106
  adding, to website header 104
  final website header composition, completing 108, 109
  Text element, creating 104, 105
Italic property 66

J

JavaScript Object Notation. *See* **JSON**
jQuery 10
jQuery Mobile library 102
JSON
  jQuery, using 15, 16

K

keyboard shortcuts
  Command+Shift+S 21
  Ctrl+Shift+S 21
Keyframes 83

L

library panel 46
Location property 64

M

Mark
  using, for animation 86, 88
menu system, Adobe Edge
  edit option 31
  file option 30
  help option 36
  modify option 32, 33
  timeline option 33, 34
  view option 32
  window option 35, 36
mobile deployment 10
Modify options
  Align 32
  Arrange 32
  Convert to Symbol... 33
  Distribute 33
  Edit Symbol 33
  Enable Smart Guides 33
mouseover command 107

N

new Edge Project
  creating 19, 20
  file structure 21, 22
  Save As option 21
  Save option 20

O

online resources, Adobe Edge
  @AdobeEdge 113
  Adobe Edge Community Forums 113
  Adobe Edge Forum 113
  Adobe Edge Preview 112
  Adobe Edge Runtime APIs 113
  Adobe Edge Wikipedia Article 113
  Edge Kingdom 113
Opacity property 64
Option + Click 83
Overflow property 65, 68

P

panels
  about 45
  actions panel 48
  library panel 46
  properties panel 47
Playback Actions property 67, 68
playback controls, Edge Timeline
  Search 81
  Time 80
  timeline options 81
Playhead
  using, for animation 84
Position property 67
properties panel 47

R

Raster image. *See* **bitmap**
rectangle elements, properties
  Background Color 65
  Border Color 65
  Border Radius 66
  Border Style 66
  Border Thickness 66
  overflow 65
Rectangle tool
  about 39, 52
  using 52, 53
Rotate property 65
Rounded Rectangle tool
  about 40, 53
  using 54, 55

S

Scalable Vector Graphics. *See* **SVG**
Scale property 65
Selection tool
  about 37, 62, 108
  element types, properties 64
  using 63, 64
size property 64
Skew property 65
Source property 67
Stage 42, 43
Stage, properties
  Autoplay 68
  Background Color 68
  Composition ID 68
  Document Title 68
  Height 69
  Overflow 68
  Width 68
SVG
  about 69, 70
  images, importing 71
symbol elements, properties
  Playback Actions 67
  scrub 68
symbols
  about 75
  creating 76, 77

T

Tag property 64
Text Color property 66
text elements, properties
  Align Center 67
  Align Left 67
  Align Right 67
  Bold 66

Font Name 66
Font Size 66
Font Size Units 66
Italic 66
Text Color 66
Underline 66

Text tool
  about 41, 56, 104
  Font asset, defining 60
  new font, testing 61, 62
  text element types 56
  using 57-59
  web fonts, using 60

Timeline controls
  about 81
  keyframes 83
  Mark 82, 83
  Playhead 82
  zoom controls 83

Timeline options
  Auto-Keyframe Properties 33
  Expand/Collapse All 34
  Expand/Collapse Selected 34
  Generate Smooth Transitions 33
  Insert Label 33
  Insert Trigger 33
  Move Playhead to Start 33
  Play/Pause 33
  Snapping 34
  Snap To 34
  Toggle Mark 34
  Zoom In 34
  Zoom Out 34
  Zoom to Fit 34

timeline options, playback controls
  about 81
  Auto-Keyframe properties 81
  generate smooth transitions 81
  Only show animated elements 81

Transform Origin property 64
Transform tool 38, 62
Transition, editing
  delay 89
  duration 89
  easing 89, 90
  end 89

U

Underline property 66

V

View options
  Actual Size 32
  Zoom In 32
  Zoom Out 32

W

WebKit 10
website header
  final composition, completing 108, 109
  interactivity, adding 104
  Text element, creating 104, 105

website header, animating
  asset import 90, 91
  General Layout 90, 91
  project setup 90, 91

welcome screen, Adobe Edge
  Create New option 18
  Open File....option 18
  Other Options options 19
  Recent Files options 18

Width property 68
Window options
  about 35
  Code 36
  Editor 36
  Elements 35
  Library 36
  Properties 36
  Timeline 35
  Tools 36
  Workspace 35

Z

Zoom In 32
Zoom Out 32

Thank you for buying
Adobe Edge Quickstart Guide

About Packt Publishing

Packt, pronounced 'packed', published its first book "*Mastering phpMyAdmin for Effective MySQL Management*" in April 2004 and subsequently continued to specialize in publishing highly focused books on specific technologies and solutions.

Our books and publications share the experiences of your fellow IT professionals in adapting and customizing today's systems, applications, and frameworks. Our solution based books give you the knowledge and power to customize the software and technologies you're using to get the job done. Packt books are more specific and less general than the IT books you have seen in the past. Our unique business model allows us to bring you more focused information, giving you more of what you need to know, and less of what you don't.

Packt is a modern, yet unique publishing company, which focuses on producing quality, cutting-edge books for communities of developers, administrators, and newbies alike. For more information, please visit our website: www.packtpub.com.

Writing for Packt

We welcome all inquiries from people who are interested in authoring. Book proposals should be sent to author@packtpub.com. If your book idea is still at an early stage and you would like to discuss it first before writing a formal book proposal, contact us; one of our commissioning editors will get in touch with you.

We're not just looking for published authors; if you have strong technical skills but no writing experience, our experienced editors can help you develop a writing career, or simply get some additional reward for your expertise.

[PACKT] PUBLISHING

Learning jQuery, Third Edition

ISBN: 978-1-84951-654-9 Paperback: 428 pages

Create better interaction, design, and web development with simple JavaScript techniques

1. An introduction to jQuery that requires minimal programming experience
2. Detailed solutions to specific client-side problems
3. Revised and updated version of this popular jQuery book

Dreamweaver CS5.5 Mobile and Web Development with HTML5, CSS3, and jQuery

ISBN: 978-1-84969-158-1 Paperback: 284 pages

Harness the cutting edge features of Dreamweaver for mobile and web development

1. Create web pages in Dreamweaver using the latest technology and approach
2. Add multimedia and interactivity to your websites
3. Optimize your websites for a wide range of platforms and build mobile apps with Dreamweaver

Please check www.PacktPub.com for information on our titles

HTML5 Canvas Cookbook

ISBN: 978-1-84969-136-9 Paperback: 348 pages

Over 80 recipes to revolutionize the web experience with HTML5 Canvas

1. The quickest way to get up to speed with HTML5 Canvas application and game development
2. Create stunning 3D visualizations and games without Flash
3. Written in a modern, unobtrusive, and objected oriented JavaScript style so that the code can be reused in your own applications.
4. Part of Packt's Cookbook series: Each recipe is a carefully organized sequence of instructions to complete the task as efficiently as possible

HTML5 Multimedia Development Cookbook

ISBN: 978-1-84969-104-8 Paperback: 288 pages

Recipes for practical, real-world HTML5 multimedia-driven development

1. Use HTML5 to enhance JavaScript functionality. Display videos dynamically and create movable ads using JQuery
2. Set up the canvas environment, process shapes dynamically and create interactive visualizations
4. Enhance accessibility by testing browser support, providing alternative site views and displaying alternate content for non supported browsers

Please check **www.PacktPub.com** for information on our titles

Printed in Great Britain
by Amazon.co.uk, Ltd.,
Marston Gate.